WHEN ENOUGH
IS ENOUGH

AVERY

a member of Penguin Group (USA) Inc.

New York

A Comprehensive Guide to

Successful Intervention

❧

WHEN ENOUGH
IS ENOUGH

❧

CANDY FINNIGAN

with SEAN FINNIGAN

Published by the Penguin Group
Penguin Group (USA) Inc., 375 Hudson Street, New York,
New York 10014, USA • Penguin Group (Canada),
90 Eglinton Avenue East, Suite 700, Toronto, Ontario M4P 2Y3,
Canada (a division of Pearson Canada Inc.) • Penguin Books Ltd,
80 Strand, London WC2R 0RL, England • Penguin Ireland, 25 St Stephen's Green,
Dublin 2, Ireland (a division of Penguin Books Ltd) • Penguin Group (Australia),
250 Camberwell Road, Camberwell, Victoria 3124, Australia
(a division of Pearson Australia Group Pty Ltd) • Penguin Books India Pvt Ltd,
11 Community Centre, Panchsheel Park, New Delhi–110 017, India •
Penguin Group (NZ), 67 Apollo Drive, Rosedale, North Shore 0632,
New Zealand (a division of Pearson New Zealand Ltd) •
Penguin Books (South Africa) (Pty) Ltd, 24 Sturdee Avenue,
Rosebank, Johannesburg 2196, South Africa

Penguin Books Ltd, Registered Offices: 80 Strand, London WC2R 0RL, England

Most Avery books are available at special quantity discounts for bulk purchase for sales promotions, premiums,
fund-raising, and educational needs. Special books or book excerpts also can be created to fit specific needs. For
details, write Penguin Group (USA) Inc. Special Markets, 375 Hudson Street, New York, NY 10014.

Library of Congress Cataloging-in-Publication Data

Finnigan, Candy.
When enough is enough : a comprehensive guide to
successful intervention / Candy Finnigan with Sean Finnegan.
p.   cm.
ISBN 978-1-58333-297-9
1. Crisis intervention (Mental health services).   2. Drug Addicts—Family relationships.
3. Drug addicts—Rehabilitation.   I. Finnigan, Sean.   II. Title.
RC564.29.F547   2008   2007049149
362.2'04251—dc22

Printed in the United States of America
3   5   7   9   10   8   6   4   2

BOOK DESIGN BY MEIGHAN CAVANAUGH

While the authors have made every effort to provide accurate telephone numbers and Internet addresses at the time
of publication, neither the publisher nor the authors assume any responsibility for errors, or for changes that occur
after publication. Further, the publisher does not have any control over and does not assume any responsibility for
author or third-party websites or their content.

Neither the publisher nor the authors are engaged in rendering professional advice or services to the individual
reader. The ideas, procedures, and suggestions contained in this book are not intended as a substitute for consulting
with a physician or other health care professional. All matters regarding the health of the subject of an intervention
require medical supervision. Neither the authors nor the publisher shall be liable or responsible for any loss or
damage allegedly arising from any information or suggestion in this book.

We dedicate this book to:

Evelyn Finnigan,
a legacy of service and compassion

and

Bob Howse,
who had the patience of a saint

CONTENTS

WHEN ENOUGH
IS ENOUGH

INTRODUCTION

My name is Candy Finnigan. I have been an adopted child, a daughter of dysfunction, a student doing hard time with the Sisters of the Blessed Virgin Mary, a debutante, a Junior Leaguer, a loyal friend, a mother, a working mother, an alcoholic, a dental hygienist, a rock 'n' roll wife, a chemical dependency counselor of adolescents, and a confidant to celebrities, stars, and strangers. But for the purposes of this book I'm a recovering alcoholic with more than twenty solid years of sobriety and years of service work—formal and informal. I'm a drug and alcohol counselor with vast and varied experience helping others to find recovery through hundreds of treatment options, challenges, and failures. I am an interventionist. And it is my passion for—and belief in—the recovery process that led me to help parents and kids, husbands and wives, and friends and loved ones of alcoholics, addicts, and the mentally ill who had realized enough was enough.

For me, it's been a long journey across the treatment landscape, which has changed dramatically over the years. I sought education, certification, and clinical work in order to ensure that the breadth of my training would complement the depth of my experience. From sober lunch programs at Beverly Hills High School, to sitting with a "wet one" after a women's meeting, from aging film actors to adolescent inhalant "huffers," dual diagnosis cases to "cutters," I've had the privilege of witnessing countless miracles as well as the lessons of tragic failure.

I enter homes where families are in crisis from drug or alcohol addiction. I lead them in a desperate, last-ditch effort to reclaim a lost loved one. They don't know me, but they need me. My coauthor and brother-in-law, Sean Finnigan, is a veteran of many such encounters as well. We want you to get to know us, we want to earn your trust, and we want to help you.

⚬⟊⚬

Intervention is both ancient and new. All societies and cultures have had a shaman, an elder, a social judge, or a religious or spiritual figure who addressed harmful behavior or mental illness in the midst of the community. Often they were women, sometimes midwives or herbal practitioners. Their solutions, incantations, or remedies were thought to have power based on spiritual authority. American Indians would try different methods to restore harmony, but if these failed, they practiced banishment. The Inuit have been known to send repeat offenders off to their own island with some provisions, a spear, a canoe, and a heartfelt "good luck." For Roman Catholics the last resort was exorcism. Christian, Muslim, and Hindu cultures alike have various forms of "balance restoring" techniques. These were often quiet, personal affairs, carried out with reverence and determination. There were times, however, when whole tribes or communities were forced to respond—sometimes harshly—to behaviors that threatened everyone. Not much has changed.

Today some 4 million people tune in every week to watch *Intervention* on the A&E cable network. What happens on the show comes closer to the real thing than any documentary series has before, but it's still only a sort of hybrid approximation of intervention. It's public, quick (due to thorough editing), and then it's over—all in an hour. The whole process could never be shown in its entirety.

Intervention, the series, shines a thoughtful light on a hard subject. That it's popular and growing reveals where millions of families find themselves: out of answers and fascinated with any idea that might work. Sean and I field scores of phone calls every week for help, hundreds of e-mails every month, and the tide is rising steadily.

As I travel around the country I meet men and women who are fans of the show. As we talk, there is inevitably a bittersweet moment: They tell me about their "lost one" and how they are dealing with their problems. If you are holding this book, interested in the help it offers, then you have joined the millions personally affected by this country's crisis. I'm sorry for our mission together but privileged to be a part of your solution.

❧

Our society is in the grip of an epidemic. It is a monster with many heads, springing from one body: addiction. The variety of substances and afflictions is bewildering, but the suffering of the families and friends of those taken have a stunning sameness: ignorance, naiveté, blame, and shame are the hallmarks of their common bond. Overstating the enormity of the addiction crisis is impossible. The reality defies imagination or exaggeration. The nature of the epidemic is systemic, and it is an indictment of our ability as a culture and a country to respond. But the particulars are personal, familiar, and paralyzing to everyone affected.

An estimated 25 million Americans are currently alcohol- or drug-dependent. The conventional wisdom is that each of those 25 million affects seven other people through familial, social, or professional associations. Let's be superconservative and cut that number in half. Twenty-five million in thrall times three people affected equals 75 million involved. If you've recently joined that unhappy group of 75 million, we want you to realize you are far from alone. That means there is no reason to proceed alone.

We can't generalize about who these addicted or alcoholic people are. Whether you embrace or deny the "disease" model is beside any practical point. I always ask families whether they prefer their loved one to be addicted or mentally ill: pick one and let's get started. The nature of dependency is ultimately uniform: the life of the lost one is diminished; they become increasingly isolated, ineffective, and eventually hopeless. The families of the lost one act as a mirror to this downward spiral, their own dynamic in turn becoming slowly and subtly deranged, as each family member is rendered unable to find any healthy perspective or rational response. They live by excuse, explanation, and denial. Under these stressors the "normal" family pattern is for each member to withdraw, either outside the home or within themselves.

Ironically, the chief activator of their fear and paralysis is love!

Introduction

If you are holding this book thinking "I can relate," Sean and I get what is happening to you, and we bring good news: the answers are in hand, actually. We promise you that the end to your personal hell is before you. We tell families a couple of things early on, things that are hard to hear but fatal to ignore: Your secrets keep you sick. Your loved one is lost to you now. What are you afraid of? And finally: how long do you want to stay sick?

☙❧

I was blessed to be delivered from my own destructive drinking through the actions of my mother-in-law, Evelyn Finnigan. She was primarily concerned for the welfare of her grandchildren, feeling that my own situation was up to me to address. In her personal search for help and solace, she had earned a "black belt" in Al-Anon (an organization for people affected by alcoholics, the family component to Alcoholics Anonymous).

She confronted her son and me in a letter, at a time when I was truly sick and tired of being sick and tired. While I refused to read her letter, my husband wrote back a defiant, attacking reply.

Our charade continued, complete with all the trappings of happiness and success, but the die was cast. Slowly our lives were unraveling. My secret drinking and the hectic pace of our life made more and more demands on me, and the effects began to tell on both of us. After a particularly stressful visit, Evelyn informed me at the airport, "You have six months to decide how to live your life, then I'll be forced to decide how to raise my grandchildren!"

Soon after that I spent my last fateful night battling booze and my life. There was not enough, and it was all too much. Dawn

5

brought surrender, and a decision to find help. I called Evelyn, and she told me she would come out but only after I had stayed several days in rehab. I entered a treatment center, completed their program, and began attending twelve-step meetings. Honestly, I entered treatment looking for some peace and quiet and to escape the guilt and fear that were killing me. Toward the end of my stay, my husband had decided to begin his own journey to recovery, so hope began to grow in our family. We both became "first timers"—people who, once introduced to recovery and sobriety, manage to embrace and maintain the principles prescribed and actions recommended and to use the resources available to them. Relapse has not been a part of our story, but that is rare. We deplore the common wisdom within the recovery community that "relapse is a part of recovery." It is not. But it is a part of addiction and mental illness, and it's a reality that needs to be recognized in all treatment modalities.

I say these things not as a note of virtue or accomplishment but in gratitude. I am sober not by any special talent but by circumstance, willingness, and desperation—all born of a belief that my life depended on all that ensued. In my twelve-step fellowship I found people like me; I heard my story being told for me, over and over. So you see that family action can make the crucial difference, when families seek the truth together from a place of resolve, love, and concern. My road back started with one letter, one woman. For Evelyn, the time for action had come: enough was enough!

As our lives were transformed and restored, our family began to heal; we regained joy, intimacy, trust, and, most important, purpose. Sean eventually became sober as well, after a lifetime spent in and out of prisons, rehabs, and some serious scrapes. We took distinctly different paths but arrived at the same place of hope and transformation. As a result of our broad and different experiences, and the clear understanding that our relief required action and a dedicated effort to help others, we found that purpose I referred to.

⚜

Sean and I have booked thousands of hours in family groups, prison panels, advisory boards, one-on-one counseling, years of service in rehabs, hospitals, crisis centers, and psychiatric facilities as advocates for the lost ones. I have performed hundreds of interventions, while Sean organized countless family groups and meetings. Through it all we have been especially drawn to the families of these degraded men and women, their children, husbands, brothers and sisters, wives, and parents. Though they are often blameless in the plight of their loved ones, they suffer in a way that is most unfair and debilitating: helplessly.

By now, we've seen it all. We know the worst and the best that can happen. We know all the stories and how they end if unchecked. There is no "new" development waiting around the corner for us. The facts of addiction, alcoholism, and recovery are knowable. All success looks the same, all failure is identical, and the similarities are constant. With this book in hand, we will be with you, advising and encouraging you. We will be your "new eyes," present and working with you. It's all of us, together, until the wheels fall off.

An astounding 80 percent of organized interventions result in the lost one accepting treatment. That is a remarkable figure, a stunning fact. Unlike every other option available to you, unlike everything else you have tried, there is a process that offers you a huge advantage. Why didn't someone tell you? Because it seems too simple, too easy, and no one gets to bill you endlessly. That's why. It is homegrown, based in action, love, and common sense—and therefore dangerous to the expert and expensive purveyors of medicine, therapy, and quick-fix promises.

We are going to guide you, prepare you, and aid you after the fact. Think about the moment you are in, right now. Do this, with us, and in a matter of days or weeks everything will change. I mean everything: your confusion, your fear, the secret keeping and silence that have sucked the air out of your home, your marriage, your life. The truth is about to be spoken out loud and repeatedly in the days ahead, and the lost one's grip on their hostages will loosen.

Together we will evoke a new dynamic around you and your life, where action spells relief. During our own recoveries we heard stories of triumph over addiction, and we began to feel reassured. We became hopeful that we were in the company of people who understood us, people with an answer. Here were people who truly wanted only the best for us, with nothing to sell or gain by our recovery. So we will find our common cause and begin to gain advantage by our numbers and our knowledge.

⚜

My life's work tells me that intervention is a profound act of love and redemption, one that works. It will stimulate open discussion of previously hidden secrets, expose lies, and clarify relationships. Through intervention, families and friends can find forgiveness and affirm the future.

After an intervention, families will relate and speak to each other differently. Expectations and resentments will gradually alter. Miracles will occur. I know, because I've been in the room when it happens. None of this is instantaneous or guaranteed. Change, real fundamental change, is slow and sure, characterized by effort and faith.

Meanwhile, some very real fears are natural: If my loved one is a doctor, pilot, minister, or has some sort of licensing, community, or professional profile, they feel that they dare not risk exposure. Just as often, the fear of gossip or awareness of someone's troubles slows or postpones the vital response that is needed. Families also resent the certainty of judgment by others. We're not inclined to open up, to reveal pain and error, and to ask others for help.

Each family member or friend who participates with you will react differently throughout the process. The mother invariably vents her grief and sorrow in tears and sobbing when she is told, "You didn't cause this, you cannot control it, and you will never cure it. This is not your fault." The shame and guilt are over-powering, warranted or not. A closed system spirals and dies by silence, pressure, and denial. The simple truth is that we are not trying to make bad people good—we are helping sick people get well.

In family groups, particularly at initial encounters with families preparing for intervention, there is an intense atmosphere of fear, nervousness, and resignation in the room. There's a belief in the pointlessness of the undertaking, a surety that the identified patient—their lost one—will have none of what is about to happen, will refuse treatment, attack everybody in the room, and run away. I've seen all that—and more.

I'm telling you now that what you're about to do will not bring about all the things you're afraid of. It will finally force everyone who matters to you to overcome fear and embrace some real hope, support, and love. How powerful for you.

By necessity, we'll borrow occasionally from the literature of recovery—the masterful treatment of early recovery, family experience, and the instruction of the twelve-step programs that apply in each instance examined in our book. It's the seminal work for anyone serious about recovery. It is practical, simple, and, most important, it works. Period. No recovery is possible in a room where the truth is feared, suppressed, or hidden. On the other hand, no life is hopeless where the truth is shared. As soon as the hard things are said and the fears faced, recovery begins.

⁂

Addictions neither respect nor spare anyone, regardless of age, station, education, or pedigree. As the issues that attend the descent into fear, failure, and, finally, forfeiture have touched my own life and family, I've seen how complex the web of challenges can become for the sufferer and, especially, for their family and loved ones. Together, in this book, we'll simplify, clarify, and begin to overcome these challenges. *Together* is the key word here. You need never attempt anything alone again, unless you choose to. If you have decided that enough is enough, we're here to help you. Let's get to it!

1.

FEELINGS ARE NOT FACTS

An Objective Look at the Problem

❧

The first step in determining if an intervention is necessary for your particular situation is to face the facts. Starting now, we're leaving behind confusion, mystery, and mythology. First we'll discuss addiction in general, and then we'll help you nail down the essential facts of your loved one's problem.

THE DESCENT INTO ADDICTION

Today, in America, hardly any family, corporation, or group is untouched by the tide of addiction or alcoholism, and their attendant psychoses. Still, families and individuals commonly react with denial. Precious time slips by and the path of the lost one narrows toward the finish line that is always the same: isolation, loneliness, and finally institutions, jail, or death. There is a primal instinct on the family's part to protect the lost one, "keep it in the family," go it alone, or simply hope for a magic wand. In the long term, none of this works, ever.

The loss of control and feeling of anxious dread that creeps through a family is a gradual progression. A system that has functioned adequately begins to break down. An emotional, psychological, and spiritual crisis deepens and the family unit begins to fragment. The entire family becomes, for all purposes, sick.

The same is true for the alcoholic and addict. In their search for an external solution to internal problems, stress, or fear, they begin to medicate. Even when their initial encounters with drugs or alcohol are recreational or incidental to social interactions, the afflicted person will repeat their use, seeking to replicate the relief and reward that was triggered by the drink, drug, or behavior. The demand for the reward begins to replace other priorities and countermands character and moral choice. Eventually any interference or delay in getting relief is not acceptable.

Your *loved* one is becoming your *lost* one.

Usually they hide their new best friend, their new love. Over time their magical slave becomes their master. We believe that only people suffering from private pain search for secret medicine. They seek immediate relief for a spiritual crisis: in a bottle, a behavior, an herb, a pill, or a powder. But the spiritual aid is counterfeit. What began as a need becomes a demand: "Change the way I feel." The lost one believes that they have hit upon a personal, secret antidote that others will not approve of or understand.

Now the sufferer is keeping a destructive secret, provoking shame and guilt but also something far deadlier—resentment.

They are forced to choose, and so they begin to isolate themselves from the very people most likely to help, those who truly love and care for them. Reality is denied and ignored. More lies are told. Tempers and attitudes shift shape as relationships are redefined.

This leads to serious consequences: arrests, professional crisis, the loss of intimacy, trust, employment, and eventually security. But the lost one is trying to escape consequences, and so confrontation becomes inevitable: It is episodic and explosive but not reasoned or productive. The lost one has become a liar, an emotional or actual thief, and is lost in a journey of deadly choices. Our father, wife, husband, grandparent, friend, lover, or child is truly lost to us, and the clock is ticking. They are incapable of meaningful human relationships.

Now the circus is in town, but nobody remembers buying a ticket. Who invited this elephant into the room? Everyone is in fear, walking on eggshells. No family wants to wake up in turmoil. No one wants to admit that they are lost or losing their lives and loved one. The "fight or flight" response dictates that all organisms under threat cither retreat and pull inward or face the threat. Naturally, families are embarrassed, scared, or overwhelmed because they are roused only by undeniable crisis, wake-up calls that are stunning and abrupt. There has been an accident, an arrest, an ER visit, or a piece of mail that reveals the shocking truth. A job is lost, a bank account emptied, a beating or an overdose plays out in front of children or friends, money is borrowed or stolen, prescriptions forged, and a parade of lies finally falls to the ground exhausted under the weight of the truth. Drama breaks out in the midst of silence. No one acknowledges what their gut is telling them: someone is dying right in front of them.

Loved ones become hostage to the disease and the needs and demands of the lost one. Families are busy changing deck chairs on the *Titanic*: the view may change, but they're still going to get wet. Everyone gets sicker.

This crisis started with a joint, a single pill or drink, one episode, easily controlled and hardly dire. What happened?

Tolerance happened. The lost one, as time and reality passed, needed larger amounts of their "medicine" to reach a soothing numbness because their system became tolerant of what was initially an insult to health. The abuse had to be learned and increased to continue its effectiveness. So, too, the family learned to adjust and cope with more failure, silence, lies, and defiance—slowly.

Most of the families I have seen wrestle with their lost one's descent into addiction or psychiatric crisis followed similar response patterns: a time of denial and adjustment, a despairing acceptance of normally unacceptable facts, an overwhelming flood of feelings and fears, the instinct to keep the situation private, secret keeping, and eventually either a crisis too big to ignore or some moment of realization—something so profound that they are willing and able to demand change.

The lost one has complicated things to a point where the family's only hope is to make a concerted, honest, and sustained effort to ward off the impending doom to all they hold dear—at a time when all involved are least able to respond. The stakes are mortally high.

The lost one has complicated things so that only a concerted, sustained effort by the family can hope to succeed. This happens at a time when all involved are *least* able to respond.

SHOULD WE HAVE AN INTERVENTION?

This is a good time to pose a few simple questions to yourself and others who are concerned about the lost one. Do you believe, looking only at the facts of your lost one's life, that there is any reason to look for change without action on your part? How long are you comfortable continuing to feel the way that you do? What has to happen before you are convinced? How long do you believe this has been going on? Are there now legal, medical, or professional crises on the horizon?

Posing questions to yourself is an excellent way of writing out the facts of the situation—as you know them—and taking objective stock of where you are in this whole process. In later chapters, we will cover in detail much of what follows here. We suggest that you read through this book before you decide to go forward with an intervention. But, as an overview, let's start with the following:

Who else believes there is a crisis? There is an old Russian proverb: if nine comrades tell you you're drunk, you better lie down. Consensus has power. Others who share your concerns and have knowledge of the problem will help in making a scary decision.

Are these facts documented, or from hearsay? Facts, facts, facts. They make us strong, resolute, and less easily dissuaded in the face of misgivings and fear.

Are there legal problems? Has there been a DUI? An arrest? Possession or domestic abuse charges? An accident? As these incidents and consequences increase in frequency and seriousness, something important is afoot. Pay attention. These things do not "just happen." Experts estimate that, on average, by the time someone receives a DUI citation, they have driven drunk over a hundred times!

Have we had enough? As you gather these facts about what life has become for you and the lost one, the real question becomes "How long will I wait? How long do I dare hesitate?"

Are there financial issues? Professional failure, firings, inability to find or keep work, the constant demand for purchasing and using substances, and concealing addiction will often being about dire financial consequences.

Are there medical issues? Besides the psychological, personal, and legal damage being done, addiction can compromise the health of the lost one.

Are there personal issues with family? The marriage? Children? Friends? Coworkers? How are each of these being threatened, diminished, or compromised? Who has observed these changes? Others in the lost one's life may have more information than you alone have gathered. The lost one, after all, has become a master manipulator.

Who is willing to participate? Think of family, friends, clergy, and coworkers. See chapter 4 for more details on who to include in an intervention.

Are there financial resources for a professional interventionist? Medical detox? Inpatient treatment? Outpatient treatment? Aftercare? We'll explain all of this in detail in chapter 3, but for now it is important to have a sense of what is possible with your own resources. Have at least an idea of what you can spend.

Do we, or can we, agree on a course of action if the person refuses to get the help offered? As you will see as we go forward, agreement and combined action is best in the face of outright defiance and refusal by the lost one. Their world needs to be challenged, their system of lies and manipulation needs to be exposed and interrupted. There is power in numbers. Conversely, as long as the lost one has even one hostage in thrall, little can be done to force the issue.

Can we help support their life while they are in treatment? For how long? Be realistic and thorough in thinking about housing expenses, bills, children, pets, and other responsibilities during the time the lost one will be away at treatment.

2.

WHAT'S REALLY GOING ON?

The Essential Facts of Your
Lost One's Addiction

❧

Now it's time to educate yourself on the substances or behaviors that are killing your lost one. We will speak plainly and urgently about the realities and unique features of each addiction or behavior. We will shoot straight from the hip with you and share all of what we know, as of this moment, to be true and important to your future

Facts are a vital part of your planning and hope for recovery. You need to know exactly what you are up against and how high the stakes are. In this chapter we'll give you an overview of your lost one's addiction, and a very broad idea of the treatment they'll require. Then, armed with what you've learned here, we'll show you how to find a treatment center in chapter 3.

Before we begin, I want to say that education is vital to your cause. This section is a primer, a beginning to your search for understanding. Go online and do additional research if you can. Talk to doctors and therapists who treat the addiction that you're concerned with. Call the national and state hotlines listed in your phone books and at the back of this book in the Resources section.

Finally, let me assure you that I have been involved in interventions that concerned every one of these addictions, afflictions, compulsions, and behaviors. Intervention is an effective and direct method of interrupting any and all of these situations, provided you do the work outlined in this book. There are no shortcuts; nor is there a better, more effective tool for change.

Intervention can be used for any problem, behavior, or addiction. Any age or sex is eligible for this kind of help. Wherever a family member or friend is suffering from worry, knowing that a lost one is in crisis, intervention is the most effective form of response I know. I would not have dedicated my life to this work if I didn't have overwhelming, sustained evidence of how dramatically it works.

SOME TERMS YOU'LL NEED TO KNOW

Before we move on, I want to define several terms that we'll use throughout the book.

Detox

This is the process of detoxification, or the removal of chemicals, toxins, and their by-products from the lost one's system.

When an alcoholic has been drinking consistently over an extended period of time, removing the alcohol abruptly and without supervision and monitoring is a bad idea. For the addict the same holds true. Physical and psychological complications and difficulties can arise. Sudden cessation provokes panic, nervous system dysfunction, brain and body chemistry changes, organ stress. It may also complicate or aggravate other dormant or existing medical conditions. Blood pressure, body temperature, immune–system, and respiratory changes will occur, as well as cramping, seizures, nausea, and sweating. In the bad old days, lots of alcoholics were subjected to delirium tremens and seizures, while addicts were forced to endure hellish flu-like symptoms, shakes, hallucinations, skin-crawling sensations, and breathless hours or days without relief.

Today, medicine and science recognize the importance of a detox procedure prior to abstinence. Some substances once thought of as "lightweight," and nonaddictive are now known to cause long-lasting, devastating periods of withdrawal. The "benzos," like Xanax and Valium, are among the worst offenders. No reputable treatment facility will admit a client without doing a thorough assessment of their case and making sure that a detox has been done. Some treatment centers work exclusively with one or several detox facilities, some programs include a detox component, and others may simply recommend several and let you choose.

Detox is essential when there has been long-term or heavy use. In general, a lost one who is early in their addiction may not need a complete medical detox, but that should be determined by a professional, a physician, or an addictionologist. The initial experience of the lost one is critical in early recovery, and any effort that encourages their progress, any action that can aid and reassure them during the crucial first thirty days, is a wise course. Physical suffering is not useful or necessary.

Inpatient Treatment

As the name suggests, this is what most people envision when they hear *rehab*. Sometimes inpatient treatment is called residential treatment. It's normally measured in twenty-eight- to thirty-day increments. The lost one goes to the facility and remains there for an extended stay. Here a staff of professionals can help the lost one address their situation and learn about the substance and addiction. And, more important, they learn how to prepare for long-term recovery. Using twelve-step program material, behavior modification, and basic life-skills components, inpatient treatment is perhaps the best opportunity for everyone to get some time and distance from old habits, old ideas, and familiar pressures and anxiety.

Outpatient Treatment

Often a first-response option for adolescents and professionals, this approach uses blocks of time, generally after-work hours, to educate and support the alcoholic or addict without removing them from their environment. Sometimes they are affiliated with hospitals, but outpatient treatment centers are often stand-alone programs, offering convenience and affordability. Sometimes the use of insurance is allowed. Outpatient programs can range from intensive programs that meet daily to those that meet less than daily.

Transitional Living, Sober Living, Halfway House

In the face of long-standing or deep addictions, legal troubles, a volatile home life, or other factors, it is best for lost ones who have completed inpatient treatment to have a transitional housing option. While they are free to work, attend meetings, and have general freedom of movement, they are also surrounded by others who share their journey and experience.

Through support, monitoring, and rules, these environments can go a long way toward helping the lost one in early recovery. Meetings on the premises, schedules, and chore responsibilities can provide a less pressurized, friendlier type of experience during the initial period of sobriety. They are often affordable, and they form a nice bridge to normal life and full functioning. Many will offer curfews, drug testing, and other useful controls or opportunities to succeed by doing, without the added pressure of fully resuming relationships and responsibilities.

These transitional living environments can be a critical factor in recovery. They are also an extra safety net for families, and a way for families to gain confidence and reassurance that their lost one is indeed recovering.

3-D (Double Deadly Drugs) Substances

This is our term for substances of particular significance because of their vicious addictive power, the long-term psychological damage they cause, the profound character of withdrawal from them, the recovery challenges they pose, and their inherently destructive nature.

ALCOHOL

Alcoholics Anonymous is a masterful book written by and edited under the guidance of A.A. founders Bill Wilson and Dr. Robert

Smith. It's the most comprehensive, authoritative work on recovery from alcoholism. It contains poignant and meaningful insights into the nature of the disease. I suggest to any and all who find themselves confronted with destructive drinking in a loved one or themselves to read through its early chapters, especially "The Doctor's Opinion." Science and medicine have basically accepted that alcoholism is not a choice or a weakness, not a character issue. Society, I suspect, quietly lags behind such progressive thinking.

My experience in helping families of countless alcoholics is an endless, heartbreaking parade of ignorance and righteous judgment by society, friends, and family. An awful lot of people still believe that people drinking themselves to death are making a sort of convenient, lazy choice. Here's what I know: whatever a person's drinking history may be, whatever the good times looked like in the beginning, end-stage alcoholism and chronic drinking have nothing of the party in them. By the time this book is important to you, the consequences of your lost one's drinking likely have become dire—dire enough to threaten their life, your relationship, and your sanity—and that of your entire family. Undoubtedly your lost one's life has begun to unravel in several ways. As a sober friend of mine says, "No one rolls into Alcoholics Anonymous on a winning streak."

Alcohol and Young People

For the parents and family of underage or young drinkers, a crisis generally involves trouble at school, a police encounter, an auto accident, failing grades, or worse. Young people used to arrive at college, or their first job and independence, and gradually establish their own drinking or using pattern. Some would fail to adjust or modify their use and proceed to fail, quietly or spectacularly. No more. Today I see young people in their early teens who have a full-blown alcohol or drug history, have established their substance or substances of choice, and are part of an integrated, sophisticated supply chain. Our children function every day in a highly charged social network. Getting alcohol or any other drug is simple, and paying for it may be a communal effort.

A lot of kids now are supplying themselves initially from the liquor at home. Most groups that party together have worked out which homes are "safe" for drinking after school, whose mom works late, which home is easiest to sneak out of during sleepovers, and unfortunately whose house has a welcome mat outside—where parents drink and drug themselves, allow parties and worse under their own roof, or reason that "I'd rather have them doing it here." I must point out here the insanity of such thinking. Any parent with knowledge of underage drinking and drug use is guilty of a felony—contributing to the delinquency of a minor—as well as aiding and abetting a more serious crime.

An ever-growing number of kids live with a single, working parent. This often results in less discipline and accountability for teens, and less intimate knowledge of friends and habits by that single parent. Our kids are also more mobile than ever before. Between the Internet, cell phones, and virtual meeting places like MySpace, they are practically independent by age twelve. They have demanding schedules with outside interests from sports to other lessons or commitments after school. Some are working part time or are off to the library or to study groups. The end result is more time away from supervision, more freedom, and a less scrutinized itinerary. Meanwhile, the bulk of their day and a large part of their nights are dominated by time spent within their peer group.

While we need not invest too much energy in numbers, some figures do illuminate current reality. Our government estimates that some 15 million young people between twelve and twenty years of age are having a drink this month. They think that about 10 percent of them are drinking heavily, and a further 20 percent are bingeing, that is, drinking to blackout or insensibility once they start. The average age for a young person to begin drinking is thirteen! By graduation a stunning 60 percent have been drunk. Girls start even younger.

Drinking is seen as a release from pressure, a celebration of communal independence, and as a mature behavior. The main result being sought is relief, an alteration of consciousness and release from anger, inhibition, judgment, or worry. In short, they seek an instant good time.

Now for some consequences: alcohol is a prime factor in all four leading causes of death in young people (vehicle crash, unintentional injury, homicide, and suicide). A full two-thirds of all date rape and sexual assault among teens is attributed to alcohol abuse. Among juveniles convicted of felonies, alcohol played a role in an amazing 60 percent of cases. For me, the most important facts are these: the younger they start drinking, the more likely they are to have sex sooner, use narcotics, smoke, fail in school, be involved in legal proceedings, and develop alcoholic behaviors. Do we need to know more?

Let me close our discussion of young people and alcohol with this: the younger a person drinks, the worse the problems down the road. The longer they are allowed to seek and find this counterfeit relief, the harder it becomes to discourage or alter their behaviors. Simple facts, but they are too often overlooked, resulting in damage to too many young lives. Act swiftly, act decisively, and do not bargain or compromise. I want to tell you something now, born from too many years of watching families fail. The number one factor in your adolescent's future happiness and success is how seriously you go forward. The hardest part of this whole problem for adults is meaning what they say, following through, and recognizing the urgency called for in the face of crisis. This disease is not going away—and it will always worsen if left unchecked. With an adolescent, you—as the guardian or parent, older brother or sister, grandparent, or concerned friend or relative—will never again have such leverage, influence, or opportunity. This is the optimal time to make a difference, a huge impact on the all-important future.

In the case of intervention and treatment for young people, the commitment on the part of the family may seem like an awful lot of work. Mom and Dad must make an effort to be firm and fast monitors, judges, and juries; a young life is at stake, and the responsibility for action and knowledge is sacred. Parents must become aware of the social and psychological realities of their lost one. They must be vigilant, relaxing only as milestones are met and trust and freedom re-earned. I strongly recommend Al-Anon meetings for the family and a constant discussion and confirming of the whereabouts of the lost one and the nature of their behavior. In short, be involved and ready to reward or sanction the results of treatment. This includes who they are with, what they are doing, how they are doing in school, and how they are acting around you.

See chapter 6 for details about treatment options and staging an intervention for a young person in crisis.

ALCOHOL AND THE ADULT

Now we're entering an entirely different scenario. A man or woman of legal age may decide when and how they choose to drink. Our leverage is reduced in some critical ways. Within the context of a marriage, a committed relationship, or a close friendship we may express our disapproval, beg for change, or try to "support" our lost one in their difficulties. But eventually we must decide what we are doing and to what end.

I want to stress here and now an essential question: how much will you take? Intervention is meant to spur openness and honesty, as well as initiate an open dialogue among all who are affected. In a situation where someone you love or care for is practicing self-destruction through alcohol, and is of age, you must first decide why you are still there and what you mean to accomplish. Your leverage is reduced to some very basic components: affection, regard, financial partnership, and your presence in the relationship. As the Big Book of A.A. says, "frothy emotional appeal seldom suffices." So, after the arguments, the scenes, the phone calls, and lies, we must return to the simple facts: this situation is beyond my control, and I cannot continue to live this way.

For an adult, drinking is a legal choice until a DUI or similar encounter with the law, or some other legalistic restraint, is present. Until that moment, even though jobs may come and go, family members fall away, children be lost, and marriages ruined, they are free to die drunk or go to prison without interference from others. You see, normal consequences have no hold on a real alcoholic, other than perhaps paying useless lip service to what they are "going to do." Usually "going to" never happens. Why? Because they are powerless in a very real way and because those around them are busily bearing the brunt of their behavior. By the time a grown person has embraced alcohol as their answer to life, the substance has made inroads, chemically, into their brain and system. They have become addicted, afraid, and resentful.

In these men and women we observe the stages of alcohol dependence: intermittent use; increased frequency; gradual dependence; the beginning of failure to maintain rituals, responsibilities, and emotional presence; mood change; gradual withdrawal from normal socialization and interests; personality disintegration; hostility and dishonesty; disregard of appearance or hygiene; loss of intimacy; loss of jobs; accidents or injury; arrests; increasing isolation; and, finally, the surrender of pretense.

There is no sudden recovery in the true alcoholic without help and work.

Unlike young people, the consequences for an adult tend to be easier to deflect initially. Adults are given more room to operate and wider latitude in their affairs because of their perceived independence and abilities. Fewer people are privy to my life details, especially if I am willing to lose those people rather than come clean, if my bills are paid, and I can function in any useful capacity. Also, an intervention on an adult alcoholic is more complicated than an intervention on an adolescent. Questions of insurance, reputation, employment, health, the marriage, and children all press in and have real weight. When dealing with the adult alcoholic, I suggest that you begin by perusing the Big Book of Alcoholics Anonymous, particularly the early sections, "The Doctor's Opinion," and chapters 2 and 3, "There Is a Solution" and "More About Alcoholism." I cannot imagine a more useful way to spend a half hour as we prepare for the task ahead.

Basically, what you will learn is that once a grown person has lost the power of personal choice—in other words, when taking that first drink has become a compulsion or obsession—they are beyond your personal aid. I agree with this. My decades of experience bear witness to this simple fact. You can help them get help if they are willing, but you cannot cure, control, or cause their drinking. Never did, never will. I mean this from the bottom of my heart. This is a deep-seated, baffling disease, and to move forward you must accept your adult lost one's need for treatment, aftercare, and vigilance. Are you seriously committed to attempting to make this the central focus of all your efforts, starting here and now?

We want to say something here about the most baffling of all alcoholics: the periodic alcoholic. Here is a man or woman that is by all other accounts a normal, responsible person. There will be occasions, however, either celebratory and public, or random and private, when their consumption is massive and their behavior completely out of character. This lost one may be limited to only a couple such instances in the early going, but they are likely to increase in frequency. The periodic alcoholic is so unpredictable that no one can know when the next binge is coming. If a man or woman drinks to blackout or demonstrates fundamental personality changes on these isolated occasions—something is wrong. Do not be fooled into dismissing these times as harmless or not important. If your lost one is a periodic alcoholic, do not be deterred in your concern. The questions are always the same: Am I scared for this person's health and mind? Am I willing to live this way? How long will I ignore this behavior and its threats to our lives?

We also want to take note of a certain type of alcoholic—the blackout drinker. A blackout drinker will, having started drinking, do so until they reach a senseless state, one that blocks out all memory of events that take place during the binge. People may drive across town or across the state, check into hotels, get married, or kill someone in an accident. Anything is possible. They will have no memory the next day. Blackout drinking is symptomatic of a loss of control and choice in any drinker. It is dangerous and will only get worse as the drinking continues. It is never a normal or unimportant event. While we see a lot of it in adolescents, it is a factor in all age groups and both sexes.

My opinion and my experience with adult recovery dictates that outpatient care is most often a kind of lateral move, designed for the convenience of insurance companies as a low-cost way out of real expense, as well as a way for the alcoholic to keep their job, marriage, and those around them off their back. I cannot think of a case of meaningful, long-term recovery through outpatient treatment alone for a true alcoholic. That does not mean it doesn't happen—just that I haven't seen it, in twenty-one years of service on the front lines. In short, adult alcoholism requires an extended inpatient treatment period of thirty to ninety days, as well as extended aftercare and a plan of accountability and maintenance agreed upon by all parties before enrollment in treatment.

For long-term use—that is, a daily, sustained habit of drinking over a period of months or years—physical and emotional symptoms of withdrawal may be severe. Symptoms range from the danger of seizure to full-blown delirium tremens, hallucination, or dementia. Detoxification must be discussed, planned for, and settled prior to entering residential treatment. Any thought of immediate cessation without supervision is foolhardy and dangerous.

I recommend a minimum stay of thirty to sixty days in a residential treatment program, followed by attendance at meetings and a solid exit plan, with outpatient follow-up by professionals.

HEROIN

Heroin is the end product of a refining process applied to raw opium to produce morphine, an extract of poppies. This extract, in its rawest form, is the number one cash crop in the world when calculated at its weight-to-value ratio. Afghanistan is currently the leading supplier to the world, and the Mexican drug cartels have become its largest distributor.

In America we see very little of the Afghan product. Most of the heroin west of the Mississippi is grown in Mexico and processed by Asian cooks employed by the cartels. The bulk of the heroin in the eastern states is of Colombian origin. Both countries became major players over the last decade, expanding their role as growers and processors by acquiring agricultural and scientific guidance from their Asian counterparts. The cartels began taking advantage of the supply and distribution networks they controlled in our country for the sale and distribution of marijuana and cocaine. Heroin is potent and highly addictive.

Today, across large parts of America, it is easily available, most often in the form of "tar," a gooey substance that is one step removed from the final processing into powder form. It is cheap, easy to smoke, and extremely strong. Many police forces are now seeing tar that is as high as 80 percent pure. It is also easy to package in small, affordable amounts, costing as little as ten dollars a dose retail. I have not found a community or group that is beyond its reach. There is no longer any accurate stereotype of the typical heroin user: old, young, professional, poor, man, woman, black, white, or striped—everybody's doing it. Last year there were roughly a million and a half visits to emergency rooms for heroin overdose or crisis. A quarter of a million people showed up at treatment centers seeking help with heroin addiction. It's a growing trend and a great profit maker for the criminal organizations that count on addicts' money to thrive. The most alarming segment of new users is the middle- to upper-class young. Obviously any use is negative, but this new market segment is growing rapidly, and as usual our response time is pitiful.

My professional experience, as well as Sean's lengthy battles with heroin addiction, point to a few simple differences between the effective treatment for heroin addiction and that for other substances.

Heroin, when smoked, is easy to slide into. It is magical and potent as an analgesic (i.e., pain-reliever) but even more insidious in the way that it induces a powerful euphoria and sense of physical, deep-seated well-being. When someone smokes heroin, the danger of accidental overdose is less of a factor, since inhaling the smoke will eventually produce enough narcotic concentration that a deep and sudden sleep will result. The obvious dangers while smoking are nodding at the wheel, handling guns or machinery, or falling down while "nodded out." Heroin suppresses our lung and heart functions as well, so choking, vomiting, or respiratory and heart failure are common sources of ER visits and death. The emotional and spiritual damage done from the moment of first use forward is, unfortunately, incalculable.

Smoking is usually done by placing a piece of the tar on tinfoil and applying flame to the underside of the foil strip. As the tar melts and heats, a thick smoke plume rises. The smoker then sucks the smoke up a straw or improvised cone. This was famously referred to as "chasing the dragon," due to the heroin sliding around the foil, necessitating the "chasing" of the smoke plume from place to place. Because heroin has become so affordable, ten dollars can get a person very high, especially if they are clean when first trying the drug. Here's the rub: smoking heroin, while seemingly a more "manageable" alternative to injecting or snorting it, is equally addictive. By the time a person uses heroin on a daily or every-other-day basis a half dozen or so times in a row, they will be symptomatic as soon as they are without a dose. Irritability, a dripping nose, some joint discomfort, and a general flu-like syndrome will begin.

Injecting heroin is far more efficient and dangerous, delivering a maximum rush quickly, as the drug is almost immediately absorbed through the bloodstream into the system. The high may initially last three to six hours, and once the main rush has subsided, it will result in a pleasant overall feeling of drugged malaise. There are obvious dangers for this method of administration: exposure to chronic and fatal diseases such as hepatitis C and HIV through the use of dirty needles, infection and abscesses, overdose, and taking into the bloodstream the impurities present in the drug.

These are all very real risks when needles are used. Users have to liquefy the heroin by heating it with water, or if it is exotic Persian or Afghani heroin, by simply adding lemon juice and filtering it through cotton. Spoons are a favorite tool for performing these dreadful tasks.

Snorting or inhaling the drug takes the longest time to elicit a high, often taking ten to fifteen minutes to reach saturation levels. The problem for the casual "sniffer" is the illusion of manageability. For years, people of all stripes have been able to effect a "casual" habit, snorting or smoking on weekends or occasionally as a celebration or a particularly "wild" adventure—a walk on the dark side, thrilling and deliciously dangerous. These people are sarcastically referred to by hard-core drug users as "chippies," due to their habit of merely chipping away at the source of their relief. Make no mistake: whether sniffing, shooting, or smoking, the simple fact is that repeated use over a period of weeks will lead to addiction.

When used repeatedly, heroin triggers the suppression of important brain chemistry, particularly the production of dopamine and serotonin, both of which are vital to emotional and physical life since they are principally in charge of emotional response and mood stabilization. Sober time must pass before even a smidgen of either is eked out again, and any use in the interim starts the user back at square one. I am talking about a minimum of ten months, and probably more like a year, before these precious chemicals are active again. Heroin use is an extreme attempt to gain relief by your lost one, and the accompanying psychological and emotional issues are unique. By choosing heroin as a source of solace, these men and women have taken a darker path.

Heroin is a 3-D substance. It is truly the Black Hole of all narcotics. It is a deadly and appealing substance, one that provokes deep-seated yearning and suffering in its subjects.

I feel that the best recommendation for heroin addiction treatment is a full-blown detox at a facility used to dealing with heroin protocols, followed by a minimum of ninety days in a residential rehab with experience in heroin addiction, with ongoing exposure to Narcotics Anonymous and the twelve-step approach to recovery. Anything less is likely to be an expensive vacation from the problem rather than a viable exercise by everyone involved in long-term solutions. Follow-up drug testing on demand and an agreed-upon exit plan and contract are vital.

The Needle

Before we move on, I want to take a moment and address the darkest side of drug addiction. Once your lost one has discovered the power of injection, a line has been crossed. The thrill of the ritual preparation of the drug, the initial puncture of the skin, the rush of their blood into the syringe is very dark and alluring. By introducing substances into their blood, the lost one is taking additional risks. The health risks are numerous, and the addiction grows faster and more intensely than in other methods of use. Injecting heroin is the single most powerful signal any human can send to their subconscious. It signifies a profound desperation and a separation. The lost one is isolated from all semblance of normalcy or self-regard.

Needle users require a lengthy treatment stay, no matter what drug is being injected, merely because of the method they've chosen. I feel safe adding an additional thirty days to any treatment option, as well as extended drug testing. Anyone using needles also needs a physical exam to test for HIV, hepatitis C, and other blood-borne diseases.

We also want to note the phenomenon of "skin popping"— injecting a drug but not directly into the bloodstream. This is neither fish nor fowl, a strange sort of attempt at maximum high without the psychological acknowledgment of how far the lost one has gone in their quest for comfort and escape. We believe that anyone who can stick a needle in their arm or leg will soon try the whole shebang and go for the vein.

PRESCRIPTION NARCOTICS

Get on the Internet and go to Google or any search engine you are familiar with. Enter the name of the drug you are concerned about and go to the Wikipedia offering; it is usually several entries down the list. Prescription drugs are often marketed under multiple names and in combinations with other drugs. At Wikipedia you'll find an excellent, plain English explanation of what they are. It is a useful exercise.

Any pill can be identified in seconds on the Internet. Simply go to your search engine of choice and type in the numbers or letters on the pill and nothing else. This will almost always work. If it does not, then enter "pill identification online" and choose a site. There are several excellent sites, and this is info you need to have. Pills.com is an excellent place to start.

I am sorry to report that the abuse of prescription drugs by young people is the fastest-growing segment in the most recent government and private sector research results. More than ever before, adolescents are "scoring" their drugs at home as their parents are supplied by the doctor. As more young people are exposed to pills, and as our aging baby boomers face a litany of aches and pains, pills are taking the forefront as a primary substance for abuse and addiction.

While doctors may caution a patient or mention in passing the likelihood of developing a "habit" after long-term use of a narcotic pain reliever, their focus has never been and probably never will be the policing or monitoring of how meds are taken. Doctors are overworked, uninterested, and certainly undertrained when it comes to recognizing and dealing with prescription drug abuse among their patients. Of 126 medical schools in America, exactly eight require units on drug and alcohol abuse and addiction. Get it? We have no ax to grind with doctors or the medical community. These problems are complicated, difficult, and overwhelming in today's modern practice. GPs are seeing an average of one hundred patients a week, spending an average of twenty-two minutes per patient—I think we can safely say that things at the doctor's office are a little hectic.

Meanwhile, we are a nation growing dependent on pain relief— and pain relievers. Managed care means seeing more patients, drug companies push incentives on prescribing physicians, and thanks to drug advertisements patients arrive in doctors' offices already knowing what they want—by name, strength, and quantity. The merging of these societal, medical, and financial factors is unparalleled in our history. The number of overdoses and ER visits involving prescription medication is rising steadily.

Let's begin with the nature of these drugs. Synthetic opioids are chemically engineered to mimic the analgesic effects of opium. Morphine and codeine are derivatives of opium. It is technically incorrect to refer to these synthetic compounds as narcotics, but our government has decided that they are to be categorized as such, so we will refer to them as such.

These narcotics act by attaching themselves to neuroreceptors in the brain, spinal column, and gastrointestinal tract. They stifle some of the pain signal, thus dulling our pain. Tolerance begins within the initial thirty-day cycle of medication. By the time the patient has been taking pain medication for thirty days, the drug is no longer as effective in relieving pain when taken as prescribed. For the abuser, "take as directed" was never an option. Tolerance is simply a fact of life for an addict, requiring heavier and more frequent dosage to achieve relief, much less get high. This means more money, more secrecy, less ability to function, and an ever-rising risk of arrest, exposure, or failure to perform. It never gets better.

For young people, pills are a magical, apparently safe, and reliable buzz. They can loot them from their family or get them from friends who do the same. They may first connect with the buzz through an injury of their own. These drugs are widely available, cheap—at first—and often first encountered under the direction of a physician. They are easier to hide than booze or other drugs and need no special preparation or paraphernalia to use. Their effects are predictable and easy to measure in terms of length of time of the high.

For adults, the allure of quick and efficient pain relief is understandable. For those who first encounter these drugs by way of a doctor as a means of pain management, the development of tolerance is inevitable. Over time it will take a higher dosage or concentration to alleviate the same amount of pain. Addiction is common among long-term pain treatment cases. I don't care who you are, if you take these drugs long enough, you have developed a dependence. A chimpanzee will get strung out on OxyContin in a matter of weeks. Don't tell me he's got private impulses, deep-seated grief issues, or poor impulse control. He's hooked due to a simple equation: time plus use equals dependence.

For men and women who encounter these drugs outside of a medical setting, they provide a wonderful addition to a drink or a joint, adding a great numbness to their buzz. For the professional, pills give a reassuring message of safety and reliability while superficially removing the stigma of being a junkie or drug addict. They are not buying them in an alley from some pusher, they get them from people just like themselves: middle- or upper-class suppliers who have multiple prescriptions themselves, access to stolen supplies, or cooperative doctors who sell direct and in bulk for profit. These pills have real advantages for people who must function and appear in control. Only an overdose will cause obvious or alarming symptoms. Under normal conditions, the user can go about life pretty much aware of what's going on around them. They will eat, sleep, drive, work, and behave, mostly, like everyone else, if a tad bit mellower.

For the aged, pain management is a huge issue. Almost all of the cases of drug addiction in seniors that I've seen have begun at the doctor's office. Their pain can be long-term, intense, and getting worse. Obviously no one is concerned when an older person is approaching death and addicted to medication. So what?

For everyone else, the question becomes about quality of life. Over the long haul, these drugs begin to affect balance, judgment, memory, speech, vision, and stomach and digestive function. They may also cause intense constipation, nausea, mood swings, and sleep-pattern disruption and depression. Since the pain is unlikely to just disappear, the problem requires a competent, attentive doctor who is aware of these factors. Most doctors are simply trying to help. Some are not.

No matter how the lost one encountered these drugs, dependence and addiction often follow. The bottom line is that there are more drugs on the horizon, not fewer. More and more patients arrive at the doctor's office knowing what they want. Thanks to advertising, the Internet, and word-of-mouth, patients are educated, demanding, and feel undertreated if they do not get satisfaction from their visit. The doctor wants the lost one to be happy and wants to be of use. So the prescription pad comes out, the system kicks in, and drugs appear at the bedside. Older people take longer to detox owing to their slower metabolism and the aging of their organs, and they need more time one-on-one with counselors. Their treatment should always be enhanced with a psychiatric evaluation and a period of therapy after drug or alcohol treatment.

These drugs are powerful, deeply addictive, and appealing. They exert remarkable influence on the subconscious, sending demand signals for months after cessation. I believe that a detox program, followed by no fewer than sixty days of inpatient treatment is a minimum requirement for recovery. Attendance at twelve-step groups is a must in my book. (Wait, this is my book.) Drug testing for at least a year afterward is prudent.

Some painkillers are worse than others. Below is a list of those I consider 3-D substances. For long-term addiction to these substances, I recommend complete detox, ninety days of inpatient treatment, followed by a transitional program with drug testing. I also recommend a yearlong contract and continued random drug tests.

- *OxyContin*. Called "hillbilly heroin" because of its devastation of rural communities in a matter of two years. Huge rings of thieves, buyers and resellers, "pill mills" (clinics that specialize in lax requirements and no actual doctor's exam, these are huge moneymakers for owners and physicians), and pushers have taken control of the market. This drug is expensive, needlessly powerful, and deadly. It sells for as much as eighty dollars for a single 80-milligram pill—roughly a dollar a milligram! I have never seen a more devastating, soul-killing addiction, or a longer, more depressing withdrawal and long-term effect. It is demonic.

- *Vicodin*. I have seen more relapses, after long terms of sobriety, from this drug than any other, bar none. It is cheap and widely available. It brings a low-level high that is both physical and psychological. Its capacity to create an addicition is powerful. The development of tolerance is quick and sure. Vicodin, like all painkillers, is now available on the Internet, so scoring is no problem. I have known cases where people were taking as many as fifty of these pills in twenty-four hours! The withdrawal is a drag, and the long-term hangover effect is impressive. For a while, doctors were handing these out like party favors. They are highly addictive, hard to kick, and require long-term treatment. I suggest a minimum of sixty days, with ninety days being ideal.

- *Morphine.* This is far away from heroin. A powerful pain reliever, highly addictive, more pure and longer acting than some drugs, this pill has real power. Morphine withdrawal is one of the classics: drippy nose, skin crawling, hot and cold waves, and a body-aching flu that goes on for weeks.

- *Fentanyl.* This is one of the most powerful, ugliest drugs I have ever encountered. Fentanyl is estimated to be roughly eighty times as powerful as morphine! It is a long-acting, intensely focused pain reliever. It is, I kid you not, available in lollipop form for those who cannot take pills or have opioid sensitivity. They also have patches designed for long-term pain relief, available in strengths that can work for seventy-two hours at a time. Obviously, to the uninitiated or casual user, these dosages and delivery systems spell trouble. I have seen some ghastly cases of addiction to fentanyl, and it is not pretty. Highly potent and highly addictive.

- *Talwin.* Often used in concert with other pills because of its ability to "boost" the effects of certain medications. The combination of Talwin with Millazine, which is blue in color, was known as "T's and Blues" or "T's and B's." For a brief time in the eighties this combination was the leading cause of overdose and ER visits due to drug crisis. It is a powerful pain reliever. It is not around so much today, but it is still available, particularly in rural settings.

We want to make clear here a couple of pertinent facts: no matter how these pills are encountered, from postsurgical pain relief to injury pain management, a chimpanzee will feel the tug of need after thirty days of constant dosing followed by interruption. The development of tolerance and the progression to dependence is a simple mathematical and biological fact. Is the monkey an addict? No, it is addicted.

All of these pills are addictive, and if you take enough of any of them, you *will* become dependent. All of them require detox if taken over any significant period of time, and most addicts are best served by a sixty- to-ninety-day inpatient program that is experienced in opioid addiction. I believe that everyone benefits from a transitional living phase at the end of their inpatient treatment. Further, I believe all substance addicts should seek out twelve-step support programs, and all partners or parents should use in-home drug tests or professional services for a year after recovery begins. These are minimum suggestions.

COCAINE

The rise of cocaine as a recreational drug, in modern times, began in earnest during the late seventies. During the eighties it enjoyed an unparalleled popularity, eventually crossing every socioeconomic and ethnic boundary. It is expensive, often costing $100 a gram. The lost one may be snorting it, smoking it, or injecting it intravenously.

It is sold as a powder, though in bulk it may be rocky, having clumped together in the refining process. For ages, the coca plant that is the source of cocaine has been a staple of indigenous South American cultures that live along the spine of the Andes mountains. Chewing the plant releases alkaloids, which produce not only euphoria but also a topical numbing effect that makes clinical cocaine useful as a local anesthetic and a precursor to medical products such as lidocaine. The main benefit derived by the Indians who chewed coca leaves over the centuries is an extended period of energy, a lack of hunger, and increased mental focus. Of course these people had enough sense to leave it at that—some leaf chewing and casual cultivation. The insanity of refining, processing, and abusing the resulting powder had to wait until the mid-nineteenth century. The first big champion of cocaine was Sigmund Freud, who saw it as an amazing tool for his practice. Thomas Edison became a big promoter and fan of the drug as well, boasting of his newfound powers of perception and his alert, energized feeling. Eventually Mr. Pemberton came along and added cocaine to his sensational new soft drink, Coca-Cola. From there cocaine began to enter elixirs and patent medicines.

We know now that cocaine causes a biochemical reaction in the brain affecting dopamine production, which effects joy, excitement, and fear—pretty basic emotional and chemical impulses. As cocaine triggers a cascade of dopamine, a powerful feeling of pleasure, stimulation, and heightened perception is induced. Chemical pathways are altered over time, and when the effect wears off, a craving begins. In laboratory settings, rats will forgo food, sex, and sleep rather than go without cocaine—and they'll even dose themselves to death.

Our peak, as a nation of cocaine users, came in the late eighties into the nineties when there were an estimated 5 million users. That number has come down, but the rise of crack, a cocaine product that is cheap and easily broken into more affordable quantities, has helped cocaine surge back into the marketplace. There are roughly a million crack cocaine users at the present time.

Because of its cost and its effects on the brain and metabolism, cocaine is a destructive and dangerous drug. Cocaine is highly addictive, though not in a physical sense: cocaine is far more insidious in its appeal. Cessation of using after an extended period of abuse leads to a psychological "crash" and a series of demands from the brain that grow more urgent, eventually leading to mild depression and lethargy. The lost one can burn through large amounts of money while becoming increasingly obsessed with more frequent abuse. They will sleep less, eat less, and become dependent in a matter of months, even weeks. This is a lifestyle drug, one that becomes a magical source of energy and inspiration.

Combating cocaine addiction involves having to ignore profound changes in brain patterns and biochemical crises. Overcoming the depression that attends stopping cocaine while resisting the panic message from the brain is a formidable challenge.

This is a 3-D substance. Long-term recovery may require extended treatment. I recommend sixty to ninety days in intensive inpatient treatment, followed by attendance at twelve-step support groups. Cocaine Anonymous is dedicated solely to these lost ones and makes an excellent addition to the recovery process. Narcotics Anonymous is also a useful and effective twelve-step fellowship for cocaine addicts.

Crack

Crack cocaine swept over America and became a phenomenon by the nineties. The South American cartels that produce cocaine had built and perfected an operation that was supplying the world in huge quantities. But like any successful international supplier, they wanted a way to expand their market. What they needed was a way to sell the small consumer a low-cost version of cocaine instead of the $100 gram of powder that was the basis for their marketing.

Crack was born. Available for as little as $5 a rock, crack is a rocklike version of cocaine, not processed to powder to be snorted but designed for smoking. It took over the ghettos first, then spread to all segments of society. The cartels reaped massive profits, and the nation grew sicker. These cartels took over America without firing a shot, enslaving millions along the way.

I doubt that I have ever seen a drug more destructive, more quick to reduce lost ones to shells of themselves. It is without parallel in our drug history. Because it is cheap and easy to use, everyone can afford it. The high is so intense, the results so rapid, that the smoker is hooked within the first several uses. Because the effects of crack are so fleeting, the rush lasting moments, crack addicts can smoke up hundreds of dollars per session. They will attempt to re-create that first hit for hours, even days on end, until they drop or run out of money.

Crack use has become an epidemic. The lost ones who smoke it are reduced to zombies, only interested in getting more and getting high. Because it isn't physically addictive, users can go weeks, even months without using. But the psychological appeal is overwhelming, so that after a long time the demand is still present.

I have seen very few people recover from crack abuse without intense intervention from family, extended supervision and scrutiny, and serious dedication to support groups. Families of these lost ones must be aware that money, even small amounts, is dangerous for crack addicts to walk around with. This recovery needs participation by a loved one, over a long period, who is willing to supervise finances and monitor the lost one's financial dealings for at least a year.

This is a 3-D substance, requiring a minimum of ninety days in rehab, transitional living plans, and dedicated monitoring of all monies for at least a year. Frequent drug tests are a must.

I want you to really hear me now: this is one of the worst destroyers in my book. I take no threat to our society more seriously than the crack epidemic. This is vicious, evil stuff. It is a devastating drug, rapid acting and extremely addictive. We have never seen anything like it in this country.

Freebase Cocaine

While it is not as common as it once was, "freebasing" is a dangerous and destructive method of use. In freebasing, an agent such as baking soda is used to liquefy and purify cocaine, removing all foreign substances and rendering it pure. When dry, the cocaine is then smoked. Pure cocaine smoke rushes into the system in a matter of seconds. This is intensely destructive to the central nervous system, brain function, and emotional stability. A lot of product can be consumed, and hours of wakefulness and tension will follow. Paranoia and aggressive behavior are common.

You can think of the treatment for someone with a freebase habit as identical to treatment for crack addiction.

AMPHETAMINES

These chemical compounds are stimulants, designed for either weight loss or boosting energy. They are commonly associated with truck drivers, athletes, and people looking for sustained energy or to curb appetite. College campuses have seen a resurgence of use, thanks to Adderall, which is commonly prescribed for adolescents to treat learning and attention disorders. These substances allow a wakeful period of some three to six hours, making them perfect for use in "cramming" sessions.

Amphetamines come in pill form and are primarily prescribed for exhaustion, dieting, attention disorders, and in combination with certain psychotropic medications for the energizing effect they produce. They are usually abused by people looking for a boost or increased ability to take other drugs or while drinking.

Amphetamines eventually suppress sleep patterns and lead to paranoia, delusion, and exhaustion. Because of these effects, there can be episodes of rage and violence as well. These are nasty drugs, often making nervous, skinny wrecks of the lost ones who use them. Amphetamines may figure in eating disorders as well. They are cheap, long acting, easy to get, and they don't take long to create dependency.

These drugs are also popular in tandem with drinking or other drug abuse. The lost one can drink more than ever, becoming a wide awake drunk. Because they heighten the senses and encourage the idea that sleep and food aren't necessary, there is potential for rapid physical decline. "Speed kills" is as true as it ever was.

Treatment requires detox and rehab. I recommend a minimum stay of twenty-eight days, followed by attendance at meetings.

CRYSTAL METH

This drug is right up there with OxyContin, crack, and heroin in terms of destruction. And here's the kicker: unlike any other drug, this one can be made in the sink in a matter of hours from common chemicals! It is cheap to manufacture and cheap to buy and incredibly dangerous.

Its true name is methamphetamine, and it is a powerful stimulant. When snorted, it causes intense energy rushes and prolonged stimulation. When smoked, it is overpowering in its effects, and even faster acting. It is often referred to as "crystal," "crank," or "meth."

Meth has been a huge moneymaker for several different groups. Organized crime syndicates associated with biker clubs like the Hells' Angels and Gypsy Jokers made massive profits throughout the sixties, seventies, and eighties by manufacturing and distributing meth. In the last decade the Mexican mafia and other Mexican gangs have moved into manufacture and distribution, bringing an efficiency and consistency to the supply chain unlike anything I've ever seen.

This drug has also created an epidemic in our country. It is so affordable and so easy to make that any idiot can do it. It took me exactly five seconds to get a recipe online and find chemical suppliers that sell the ingredients! Meth users are obsessed with the effects of the drug and soon become a part of the lifestyle. Sleep is not necessary; nor is food. Meth users are known as "tweakers" because of their habit of staying up for days. They'll become involved in pointless hours of taking things apart and rebuilding them, messing with drawings or machines, or cleaning the house with a toothbrush at five in the morning.

Within the gay community, meth has enjoyed a resurgence, becoming part of all-night sex encounters as a result of the drug's ability to allow long-term, desensitized erection and delayed orgasm. It has therefore played a role in the spreading of disease and violence.

I have not seen anything like this drug for sheer destruction in minimal time. It is quick to take over the minds and spirits of a lost one. All sorts of mental illness can result from extended use, and the onset of addiction is rapid. Meth abuse, more than perhaps any other drug use, is associated with violence—guns are a common interest of the meth culture—paranoia, schizoid breaks, mental collapse, and physical deterioration. And meth is like cocaine in that lab rats will forsake all other stimuli in order to get more.

I cannot overemphasize the seriousness of the meth problem in America. It is a scourge in our communities. Young and old, men and women, no one is immune to this plague.

This is 3-D substance. The cessation of use is followed by prolonged depression and a dulled, lifeless affect for months. I recommend ninety days of inpatient treatment and an extended transitional phase, followed by sustained drug testing and scrutiny, such as constant observation of sleep patterns, energy levels, and mood swings. This is bad stuff, people, and fast acting.

THE BENZOS: XANAX, VALIUM, AND THE REST

Once thought to be fairly innocuous antianxiety drugs, these compounds were amazingly popular with housewives, professionals, kids—something for everybody. Valium was the original champion of the "quick little helper" movement in psychiatry and medicine. This little pill became a cultural icon, promising relaxation and a soothing calm.

Unfortunately, it is addictive and quickly needs increased dosage to continue delivering relief. The comedown from sustained use is nerve-wracking and debilitating. Anxiety, fear, and a shaky falling-apart feeling can go on for months. Xanax, Atavan, Klonipin, and Valium require extended and careful detox.

If someone seems unusually sedate, sleepy, or unable to track conversation, you might consider these drugs to be the cause. Extended sleep and memory loss may also tip the scale toward these drugs. Younger people frequently combine them with alcohol for instant oblivion.

Xanax was next on the scene, and it has swept the nation. Kids use it alone or in combination with alcohol, pot, or other drugs. It is overprescribed, widely abused, and easy to find. It has also become a kind of secondary rape drug. Users can experience extended periods of blackout and amnesia.

This drug not only requires a long detox but needs treatment and monitoring for some time. A sixty-day stay is optimal, and drug testing should continue for months. The psychological dependence can be overwhelming. Because it involves anxiety and the central nervous system, stopping abruptly is a nightmare. Medical monitoring is a must. I encourage you to seek a professional therapist or psychiatrist for consultation.

OVER-THE-COUNTER DRUGS

Young people around the country have discovered the cheapest and most convenient high of all: over-the-counter (OTC) cold and flu medications. These drugs are dangerous and unpredictable. Most are designed for cough suppression or as a sleep aid, and they are used in both liquid and pill form. They are often combined, and the amounts taken can be deadly to adolescents.

Drugstores are reluctant to place these medications behind the pharmacy stand, and so anyone is free to purchase them without attracting attention. The high is intense, and both psychological and physical.

On this scale the abuse of these medicines is a relatively new craze. Teenagers can seem disoriented and remote, or energized and agitated. They may have a fever, tiny pupils, and shortness of breath. Their faces may flush and you may observe intense sweating or shaking.

These symptoms require an immediate trip to the ER. While we were writing this book, several teens died from these drugs within a few weeks of one another. You cannot deal with this drug like any other problem. The first use could be deadly. Extended use has so many repercussions that we don't even know yet what to expect—from cramps, internal hemorrhaging, and vomiting to hallucinations, respiratory failure, and seizure. These drugs are trash and physically destructive.

Treatment needs to be home-based and behaviorally focused. Traditional treatment can be effective, but parents must focus on the here and now. Visit the ER immediately when the above-mentioned erratic symptoms or uncharacteristic illness appear. Do not wait. Then concentrate on paying attention as you lay down a new regime in the home including close scrutiny, control of movement, supervision of your lost one's associates. In addition to this parental intervention, your child may need extended therapy. Unfortunately, there is no drug test available for detecting these substances.

INHALANTS

Abuse of inhalants is similar to meth and OTC drug use in that it is based in common household or industrial substances.

The lost ones who use these products are known as "huffers" because the common method of use is to soak a rag with the substance and hold it over the nose and mouth while inhaling deeply. The result is a break with physical and mental reality for a period of seconds or minutes. This is destructive, scary stuff.

In adolescents, the use of industrial compounds such as solvents, glues, and other cleaning agents is a result of easy access and ease of use. Not much time or money is needed, and the lost one can use the product anywhere since all they need is a rag. The effect is fast and powerful: a disconnect with reality, lightheadedness, and intense confusion.

In addition to industrial solvents and compounds, nitrous oxide and amyl nitrate are enjoying popularity as well. Nitrous oxide is used by dentists for the "sleep" method of dentistry. It is easily available in "whippets," a bottle-shaped cylinder the size of a finger. When the pressurized gas is released by puncturing the cylinder, the outrushing gas is inhaled. A wild, disorienting rush follows, with a high lasting several minutes. Amyl nitrate is a compound made into a solid cake, the size of a firecracker. When the cake is snapped in half, the compound is released. Inhaling causes a massive jolt to the heart and a rush of intense energy. These were used in boxing and sports, as well as medicine, as a way to revive people from unconsciousness. They are both dangerous. Last year's annual NIMH (National Institute of Mental Health) survey of drug use and drinking among adolescents showed that the sector showing the largest growth was inhalants. Among eighth-graders an alarming 17 percentage had used inhalants. Besides solvents, gasoline, and the compounds described above, there is one more category of chemical inhalants that need our attention: common household products.

The most convenient sources of mind-altering chemicals for kids are whipped cream canisters, computer spray cleaner, and nail polish remover. Toluene is the active in many of these industrial household substances. They can cause everything from brain shrinkage to bone marrow loss over the long term and oxygen deprivation, heart arrhythmia, and memory loss in the short term.

Research has shown that any exposure results in the disruption of normal brain function. Because of their ready availability and the short time needed to get high, the abuse of inhalants is difficult to gauge and virtually impossible to prohibit or police.

I recommend a traditional response with some additional psychiatric help. If curfews, monitoring, therapy, and time do not work, then I recommend inpatient treatment. While rehab may be useful, the main point here is a family response: scrutiny and structure, with constant attention paid by the parents.

CLUB DRUGS AND PSYCHEDELICS

This category of drugs are difficult to assess, since their origins are varied and their effects are not well understood. There is very little research on the long-term effects of use, and less about their biochemical interaction with brain function.

Some of them, like Ketamine and PCP, are used in veterinary medicine and aren't meant for human consumption. All of these drugs are popular with young people and are associated with prolonged mental states of euphoria and heightened tactile awareness. They are thought to enhance sex and open up doors of perception that are mystical and stimulating. Any young mind would be excited by such a sales pitch. There is a subculture that has flourished around these drugs. GHB, PCP, Ecstasy, and MDA are part of the "stay up all night and feel amazing" group of social drugs.

These drugs are unpredictable and can be deadly. They are easily bought, easy to conceal, and addictive. GHB is popular in clear liquid form and is often carried in a bottle used for water, Gatorade, or other commercial drinks. There is a lifestyle growing around the nocturnal use of these drugs. They are used as a way to abandon oneself to the music, beat, and crowd experience at dances or "raves"—all-night parties that are spontaneous and intense social settings. All of these drugs have a profound effect on brain chemistry, and repercussions of their use are currently unknown. Since they are clandestine substances, their manufacture is unsupervised and their quality or purity, as well a dosage strength, are impossible to guess.

These compounds when abused over time require detox and medical monitoring. A traditional rehab or inpatient program is a good idea.

LSD, mescaline, peyote, magic mushrooms, and their ilk are psychedelics. So little is known about these drugs that understanding their effects, short- and long-term, is not possible at this time. They cannot be good. Particularly in adolescents, exposure to powerful mind-altering drugs is dangerous. They can lead to a disconnect from reality, behavioral problems, learning difficulties, personality disruption, emotional and psychiatric trauma, and paranoia. While not classically addictive, their long-term use may be harmful.

Each of these drugs is mentally disruptive and dangerous. Their use requires parental intervention or the attention of a loved one in a traditional sense—that is, listen, watch, and pay attention to schedule, friends, and mood. Start with behavioral methods—keeping control of your lost one's schedule, mobility, and associates. If traditional methods fail, I recommend psychiatric treatment. Seeing a psychiatrist or therapist on a weekly basis may begin the process of better decision making for the lost one. I see little point in using traditional rehab for these drugs.

COMPULSIVE BEHAVIORS

Compulsive behaviors offer a range of symptoms and problems, with certain commonalities. Symptoms look very similar, and treatment options are similar as well. Here I'll discuss the compulsive behaviors I see most often.

Gambling

While addiction is easy to dismiss as crazy or self-destructive, gambling addiction is one of the most difficult to understand from the outside. Drug addicts get a prolonged, chemically engineered result each time they partake of their drug of choice, lasting hours. Alcoholics get a measurable high based on how much they drink.

Gamblers experience a rush that is difficult to quantify, impossible to predict, and mystifying to those not hooked. For most substance addicts, the amount of money that can be spent is at least limited by how much can be ingested over any given period of time or by how much will result in death. No such physical limit exists in gambling. As long as someone will take your bet, extend you credit, or exchange collateral, you are capable of betting your entire worth, assets, future debt, in short, your life—in moments!

Not only is this insanity legal; it is widely advertised, romanticized, televised by ESPN and other cable networks, and available to anyone with assets. The next level is even more distressing: taking your business onto the street, dealing with bookies, lowlifes, and, let's be honest, *dis*organized crime. The fact that the gaming industry has been able to portray itself as the savior of Indian peoples, bringers of jobs to depressed communities, and as an overall responsible industry, only completes the sad charade of respectability and harmless fun. Las Vegas went through a brief attempt at fashioning this loss, grief, and manipulation into a package of family fun!

The top two moneymaking businesses on the Internet are pornography and gaming: the twin towers of corruption, crime, and legalized stupidity. Because of the massive profit being generated, they are an unstoppable market force. The prevalence and ease of access to the Internet brings to gambling forms a terrible double whammy: convenience and instant opportunity to lose—and lose big—disguised as a harmless video game. This is a serious, rapidly growing industry, based on an insidious, deadly addiction, one that has perhaps the fastest rate of destruction of any we'll discuss. I can't waste our time and energy now on a much-deserved opinion piece against the entire bunch.

An unfortunate aspect to gambling addiction is the power of that first "big score." Many times we hear the story of how the "real" trouble began after a particularly big winning streak or a sizable single triumph. Winning has a power to deliver a massive adrenaline jolt while contributing an emotional kicker that confers a grandiose sence of power in the winner. "I am powerful, lucky, and destined for winning." Nothing is worse than the curse of "beginner's luck"—that early, honeymoon experience so many gamblers experience.

The usual constraints and fiscal cautions of normal life aren't necessary for the magical winner. The inveterate gambler is hooked on that first high, chasing it forever, always sure that the answer lies in the next big wager. The highs and lows become devastating, eventually creating that dreaded cycle of bet, lose, mourn the loss, swear off, lie to those directly concerned, refuse to face the truth personally—and bet again, hoping for the "luck" that has eluded them, all of this repeated ad infinitum. Something that started small and gave pleasure has become an obsessive need to win. The gambler has transferred his or her sense of self, of worth and accomplishment, to a senseless process that has taken on special meaning.

The end result is, in many ways, identical to all other addictions but significantly different in the ways we have described. It is rare for a person to casually share with an acquaintance that they smoked a little crack this morning or that they are planning on knocking off a little early to catch up with their heroin dealer. Most people would be uncomfortable announcing to their office peers that they had a little vodka for breakfast. Not so with gambling, online or off. Society is not shocked by a mention of a wager; nor are peers alarmed when a friend says they're headed for the track for a day of racing and fun. See the difference? Especially among the under-forty crowd, online and casino gambling enjoys a very sexy image. James Bond was a baccarat fan, and everyone loves a lottery winner's story. The dream of reward for risk taking is eternal, and in the case of gambling, having the nerve to "toss the dice" is seen as icy courage. Mark Twain described gambling as a tax on ignorance. Sean and I agree with Mr. Twain, while also understanding that this problem has become deadly serious.

The final difference I need to discuss here is the nature of gambling from a treatment perspective. While even our narrow view, as a society, of addiction acknowledges the possibility of the disease model, most civilians have a difficult time grasping compulsive gambling as a "legitimate" disease. Outside of the illusion of potential profit, there is no useful application for the act of gambling. In other words, narcotics are useful to medical practice, and even heroin has a scientific application. More so in the mind of the general public than any other addiction, gambling gives the appearance of being a question of character and choice. The application of the twelve steps of recovery, as advocated in the literature of Gamblers Anonymous, is the most promising treatment modality that I know of. In these meetings, fellow sufferers will not raise questions of character or moral choice but rather extend a welcome and encouraging hand, along with some real understanding. It is clear to me that any time a man or woman begins to lie about their gambling, illness is present and crisis is brewing.

Having dealt with several cases of gambling addiction and the heartbreak and damage it causes, I can say to you that I know of no addiction that can more quickly destroy a person, their family, and future. None. It breeds isolation and dishonesty in the gambler, and overwhelming insecurity and fear in the mate or partner of the gambler. Phone calls, the mail, and visits by strangers harbor an unknown and constant threat. In the final stages there is often the threat of death or beating at the hands of criminals. All of this is brought into the home under the cover of recreation and luck.

My recommendation for treatment is immediate surrender of financial matters to a mate or accountant, immediate transparency in all financial dealings, the placing of assets and financial instruments in the hands of whoever is present and still willing, and a total reckoning of all debt, legal or otherwise. More than almost any other disease, this one demands total disclosure and surrender of independence by the sufferer. For families and friends, the road ahead will call for a real determination to hear all the bad news, accept the financial facts, and get started on the solution. The average debt profile for a newly responsible gambling addict is six to seven figures, and the debt usually encompasses the home, insurance policies, and all other assets.

Unfortunately, at this time of financial ruin, the treatment takes additional funds. The good news is that Gamblers Anonymous and the National Council on Problem Gambling are both amazing groups of dedicated professionals. Some treatment programs will sharpen a pencil and beat the bottom line to death trying to find affordable treatment for clients, as well as shooting straight about the facts and myths around the disease. There are ten centers in the United States dedicated solely to the treatment of gambling addiction. They're listed in the Resources section in the back of this book. Contact them immediately and tell them your story. They will guide you to the nearest support group.

I recommend a minimum of sixty days of inpatient treatment

and a well-defined transition to an outpatient program heavy on meetings and accountability. Transitional living may be best in these cases. And nothing is more important than an ongoing family-group component. Make sure that any treatment center has one.

❧ *Beth's Story* ❧

Beth was a nineteen-year-old girl who dropped out of school in a gradual sort of way. Her parents had raised three other girls, all much older, and Beth was different from them. Because her parents were older (in their fifties) and both worked, she was able to get away with more. She began to skip school, and then she just stopped attending. She spent hours locked in her room playing video games and smoking pot.

When her parents realized she wasn't attending school, they confronted her but were unprepared for the emotional and furious response they got. She would not and could not stand her school, her teachers, or the other students. She was socially inept and increasingly private and unpredictable, either sobbing or giggling—sometimes in the same breath!

The bewildered parents suggested she study at home for her GED and she agreed. Over time it became obvious she was not studying, as she failed the test three times.

Finally, they reached out to me. Because the family was spread out across the country and the older siblings didn't have any real knowledge of Beth's behavior, and because of the parents' age and naiveté about drugs, a nontraditional intervention was needed.

We began a time of research and preparation. I was able to convince them that the pot use was not really the primary concern. The behaviors of withdrawal, hiding out in her room, dropping out of her life, and her obsession with endless hours of video game playing were all indications of underlying mental illness. We located a program that offered a dual track of psychological evaluation, addiction treatment, and treatment for the underlying obsessive behavior.

In the meantime, Beth's mother took her on a long planned trip to Scotland to visit family. She soon discovered that Beth was wracked by anxiety and fears of all kinds. Her mother grasped, for the first time, how her daughter needed pot to self-medicate her many phobias.

When they returned, her parents toured the facility and liked it. They decided to first enter her in a ten-day segment to secure the assessment and recommendations of the center, while seeing if Beth would go and stay.

Although she was not happy with the idea, we were able to stand firm and convince her to go and check it out, with the understanding that she would stay for the ten days or face the consequences.

The first few days were rocky, but her parents maintained their determination, and despite some frantic calls home, Beth stayed. Because Beth had never been exposed to this kind of environment—a group of her peers with similar issues, a staff dedicated to helping her understand what was happening to her, relief from parental pressures and the pressures of isolation—she slowly opened up.

When her ten days were up, she insisted on coming home for a family wedding. It was obvious that the social pressures with

(Continued)

family and the outside world were too much for her. In a matter of days she was smoking pot again. After some reasoning and another round of firm "suggestions," she agreed to return to treatment. Beth enrolled in the twenty-eight-day program and began to respond to both of the tracks of her treatment, addressing her drug use and the primary emotional illness that provoked it.

I know that Beth's success could not have been possible in a traditional rehab setting. She and her family really needed the psychiatric expertise available in the facility they chose, for diagnosis, treatment, and understanding all that was involved. They have all benefited from the time apart and have learned a great deal for the future.

Today, with the help of proper medication and an ongoing therapeutic aftercare plan, I am pleased to share with you that Beth not only secured her GED but is studying botany at a state university.

There is great reason to hope that she will never retreat from the world again.

Internet Abuse or Obsession

The lost one may use the Internet for a variety of behaviors. They may gamble online (see above), losing thousands of dollars in no time at all, from the comfort and privacy of home. Their life begins to revolve around risk and reward, all at the speed of light.

The lost one may use the computer for sexual thrills, either to meet and exchange sexual conversation and fantasy with strangers or to arrange sexual encounters. They may access pornography and download or view sexually deviant or perverted material, from child pornography to rape and incest photos or films.

Your lost one may go online to buy or shop for items as part of a shopping or spending addiction. The online auction services are a perfect one-stop facility for endless browsing and buying. This makes their behavior easy to perform and conceal. Just point and click, enter your credit card info and *voilà!*

Chat rooms and other sites offer the opportunity to meet and talk with others who share a compulsion or obsession. You can buy drugs, download porn, place a bet, find fellow fetishists, shop for furniture, learn how to manufacture meth, and find DeathStar video game players—all in the same hour. Video game addicts are not just kids anymore. Lots of adults find the imaginary life on the Web more appealing than the real world. People have become lost in Second Life, Sim City, MySpace, shopping, online gaming, fantasy football, and gambling at an alarming rate. These phenomena are relatively new, and we as a society haven't figured out how to respond.

Each of these addictions draws the lost one away from relationships, problems, work, children, responsibilities, and reality. They affect finances and general mental health in a new and disturbing way. All of these will require treatment of some kind, whether therapy, counseling, or psychiatric attention. These online obsessions or addictions do not have simple answers. You'll need to begin researching by phone and on the Internet, searching out facilities familiar with each phenomenon. Rehab is better than no response, but counseling is a must.

Cutting and Self-Mutilation

Once thought of as primarily an adolescent compulsion, cutting is a classic "cry for help." While cutters may not be suicidal, there is a danger of these ideations developing. Often cutters have been the victims of trauma: from sexual molestation, emotional or physical abuse, abandonment, or undiagnosed mental illness. While cutting is often done by girls, I am seeing more males involved. Cutting may be one of several symptoms of psychological disturbance in an adolescent. Often this behavior masks a stress response to abuse, sexual assault, or sexual identity confusion. Cutting may also be a standard cry for attention. There may be suicidal ideation.

A qualified psychiatrist is a must—these lost ones need immediate psychiatric attention. In the face of a cutting incident, parents need to launch a frontal attack: psychiatric consultation, a complete psych evaluation, and immediate counseling. A plan must be assembled quickly. If you are considering wilderness programs (see chapter 6) or rehab, the treatment center must be geared toward these particular young people. You'll want to seek out those who specialize in these behaviors.

Pornography

The lost one who is addicted to porn is a troubling case. I don't claim to understand this obsession, but I encounter it often. I believe most of these compulsions occur in cases where several addictions are present. This is referred to as cross-addiction. It is common. Pornography addiction, for instance, is often found in meth addiction, club drug use, cocaine, and crack addiction. This compulsion requires secrecy and disengagement from other relationships. The lost one feels shame and resentment of those from whom they must hide their needs. This is a complex situation and one that is understandably scary for anyone in love with such a lost one.

I do not want to underestimate the seriousness of this problem. A stay at rehab—one that understands these behaviors—is a good idea, but the real point is the need for trust and understanding. Attention must be paid to the habits and desires of the lost one. Computers must be monitored, schedules changed, access denied, and you must constantly confirm that they are not relapsing. The lost one should be in long-term counseling, at least a year of it, and all concerned should know the facts of how, when, and where this behavior was practiced. Again, the facts are important—not your feelings about them.

Eating Disorders and Morbid Obesity

Eating disorders were once the exclusive domain of women. That is no longer true. I am seeing more adolescent boys, athletes, and professionals obsessed by appearance and weight. This is primarily an addiction of control. The various forms of this disorder range from starving or bingeing and purging to dangerous weight gain. The physical dangers are chronic and numerous, while the psychological damage is profound. Food, after all, is the stuff of life. This is among the most expensive disorders to address because of the medical component that is an absolutely essential part of treatment. Waste no time in addressing any of these addictions, as they are deep-seated and subtle in their onset. The privacy of the bathroom is sacrosanct in our culture, and it is one of the rooms that becomes a focal point of this disorder.

I recommend psychiatric intervention. Find an expert psychiatrist, psychologist, or counselor who is familiar with this disease. They are everywhere. These facilities and experts can give you a full rundown on the care and aftercare recommended.

Plastic Surgery

In this addiction, the lost one becomes addicted to altering their appearance and often to the drugs that accompany surgery. This is costly and extremely dangerous. The physical risks are obvious, but the psychological harm is beyond measure. This is one of the most fundamental compulsions of all: a need to change the actual features of the body, not through effort or diet but by graft and scalpel.

I recommend psychiatric intervention. As with all of these addictions, there are psychiatrists and counselors who are familiar with it. They are not hard to find. Begin by calling psychiatric and medical facilities advertised online or in the phone book. Do the due diligence we described: start with a call, tell your story, follow their lead, and begin comparing your options.

⁂

For each of the addictions mentioned in this chapter, the process looks about the same. Familiarize yourself with all the information you can glean either online or by phone. Call all relevant organizations or support groups. Educate yourself, then the others involved. Follow the advice of professionals, doctors, therapists, and those you speak to at facilities. Take the time to check out facilities as much as you can. Consider the cost of the different treatment choices and discuss them with those involved. With a sustained effort, all of this can be done in days, a week at most. Be determined and persistent. Make a decision and stick to it. Something positive will happen. I guarantee it.

3.

NOW THAT YOU KNOW

Choosing a Treatment Option

❧

Now you know what is really going on in your lost one's life. From here on in, this book is aimed toward the day that your family's spiral stops: intervention day. In this chapter, we'll take stock of our needs and start tailoring our treatment plan.

The parent, spouse, friend, or employer of an adult in crisis bears a great responsibility. Approaching a kid, one that you gave birth to, raised, loved, and financed holds a certain psychological advantage—and we'll discuss this in chapter 6. Since the Magna Carta, however, adults who are lost have a secure knowledge that they have "rights." Any addict or alcoholic faced with a unified group of former hostages now out of the trunk and determined to effect change will quickly assert these rights. Among these are the right to tell you to take a hike.

Herein lies the great unease that is awakened in all of you who contemplate intervention. So-called grown-ups have the power of choice and are quick to assert it. Most will choose their poison over your love as long as they are able to isolate each family member, keep everyone off balance, hold a job, avoid jail, and manipulate those closest to home.

That, however, is a lot of work. As their world shrinks, the lost one begins either to grow more frantic in their efforts to hide or to retreat further into their own hell. The time that has passed as your own crisis grew—to the point that you've recently made a decision to do something—is in your favor now.

The suffering of the lost one, whatever it looks like to you, cannot be a picnic to live. You have decided to make a profound demonstration of what love and mental health look like in a family determined to recover. There is an amazing power in real love. I understand the trepidation, the fear that you are feeling.

Take heart from all that you have learned and all that I have learned over the years: intervention, the way we are going about it, can work where almost nothing else will. Let's run through our options for treatment.

OUTPATIENT VS. INPATIENT

The portrait of the average citizen walking into a rehab facility this minute somewhere in America is of a white male between the ages of thirty and forty, insured, employed in a job that pays him over $65,000 a year, and with one child at home. He will stay for twenty-eight days. I only wish I thought he was going to stay sober.

All of the good news in science and medicine, including new

drug and behavioral therapies, encourages what I call "spin-dry" psychology. I give it that name because of the rise of the twenty-eight day medical or social model programs that sell the idea that this magical number of days, combined with a financial commitment from an insurer, equals mental health for all and freedom from addiction or mental illness. We'll spin 'em dry and send 'em home humming! It is of course the result of the belief that payment to a professional means a quick solution to the problem. Unfortunately, life is seldom so neat.

For those of you about to intervene on an adult from early twenties to retirement age, the process is at its most charged. Here you are dealing not with the future of a young and vulnerable mind awash in influence and a desire to fit in or find themselves. You are up against a mind and personality already granted independence and fully formed, adults free to destroy themselves if they choose. Your marriage, your children, your finances, and your reputation are on the line. Legal and financial institutions are not as forgiving of adult behaviors, and here the record is permanent. I know that the stakes are higher and you may get only one shot, so we will plan to make it your best shot.

Intensive Outpatient Treatment

For working professionals, this is the number one favorite. It's easy to understand why: they are working with doctors, have easy access to the facility, insurance will pay for both the detox and the therapy, they can continue to work, Human Resources is bound to cooperate (the first time) in ensuring their job is secure, and here's the biggie—everyone gets off their back!

There is a great deal to recommend outpatient treatment, particularly for a lost one with no prior treatment history, a short-term drug or alcohol problem, psychiatric needs that do not require hospitalization, and as a substitute for jail time or suspended sentences resulting from DUI citations. These are all good reasons to take a look at what's available in your area and what may be covered by your lost one's insurance. I understand how big a consideration the convenience, affordability, and the ability to keep working are in deciding how to proceed. However, I strongly discourage the use of this option in cases of long-lived addictions or abuse; deep-seated emotional problems; suicidal or depressive diagnoses; a long history of prior treatment; dual diagnoses; and gambling, Internet, eating, or sexual disorders. I simply find the application of such half measures ineffective and a waste of precious time and money in the face of these other factors.

As we discussed in chapter 2, outpatient treatment is a series of meetings and workshops, attended after working hours, sometimes several times a week, sometimes every evening. Professional therapists and counselors do basically the same work that would take place in inpatient settings but without the constant social reinforcement or support found in the continuous, controlled environment offered at inpatient programs.

The main factors involved in your choice are these: Can the time and expense involved in inpatient treatment be spared? Is my insurance applicable? Is the addiction long-term and deep-seated? How much damage has already been done? Is there a legal case pending? A physical or emotional crisis? What is the attitude of the lost one? In cases of short-lived or occasional abuse, or if the lost one absolutely cannot leave at this time, then outpatient treatment is a viable alternative. In the face of the 3-D substances or of long-lived and deep addiction, inpatient treatment is the best option.

❧ The Two-Year Man ❧

Sal was a forty-three-year-old man, down on his luck and losing his family, a large Italian family back east. They were a close family, not wealthy but proud and hardworking. Sal was an alcoholic. He drank heavily and constantly.

Donald, a former coworker of Sal's, called me to find out what could be done. There were no financial resources for either intervention or treatment. After many calls I guided and directed Donald through the preparation and staging of an intervention for Sal. Donald was a warm and special man. His concern was strong, and his resolve was really something. I learned that Donald's father had been an alcoholic, and I felt that Donald was doing this for both Sal and his dad.

Donald took the ball and ran with it every time—no order was too tall, no task too much. He was "the leader" in every way. He contacted the family, coordinated them, found state-run rehab at no cost, and began to plan the big day. There was a monthlong wait at the rehab center, so he used that time to line up all the details.

Sal called his mom back east once a week, so when the time came, she invited Sal to Sunday dinner and he accepted. Donald arranged for a sibling to pick Sal up and drive him to the family home.

(Continued)

Sal was overwhelmed when he was met by his whole family, and deeply touched by their forgiveness, concern, and love. From his parents and his nine siblings to his own teenage children, the entire family embraced him. One man sat alone—the man whose love for a fellowman, one suffering a slow alcoholic death, had made this miracle possible for an entire family.

Sal loved his newfound life. He entered a facility in New York State that offered long-term treatment with transitional living. He prospered, and after a two-year journey he was offered a position on staff! He is now a drug and alcohol counselor, and he just returned from watching his oldest son participate in an international sporting event. He and his family enjoy a life that once seemed impossible.

It was this intervention that made me begin to believe a book might help people.

Inpatient Treatment

Asking someone you love to go away is against our emotional intuition. We like to believe that we have the power to solve problems, to change people, to help others recover. We may be able to support, encourage, even help make such recovery possible—but that's it. We did not make them sick, we will never make them well.

You are capable of doing everything possible and prudent to give your lost one the best chance at a happy life. That's why professionals, given the opportunity to have a client's undivided attention, having weeks of uninterrupted time to teach and listen, guide and support, may be your best option.

The role of an extended inpatient treatment center is to remove the lost one from their normal environment and detoxify their physical system while helping them overcome the trial of withdrawal. The facility will further introduce them to information and processes that will enable them to live without resort to self-administered chemical or psychiatric relief. Their time away also helps them face and accept the truth of their situation, and to do this while preparing them for reunion with their families and responsibilities—all in a matter of weeks.

Sound reasonable? To minimize the trouble ahead, to pretend that a "spin-dry" twenty-eight-day approach is sufficient, and to fail to acknowledge the spiritual, emotional, and mental components of recovery is to court disaster. All of the 3-D are identified as such for a simple reason: years of working with them and observing which approaches work most often, which invariably fail, and what the differences are has convinced me of the severity and depth of these addictions and the issues and complications they bring into play for the sufferer and all involved.

A lot of these facilities and programs will wind up being more costly than you would hope, or they may not be covered by insurance or may be far away, or may have a waiting list or other features that seem less than ideal. Often the better programs will insist on the family having little or no contact during the first thirty days, or they will have restrictions on phone calls or mail. So what? Has the ability to see each other or use the phone solved anything for you and your lost one so far? Has the constant presence of an addict or sick person in your life been a good thing lately?

What I'm suggesting to you is dead simple: do something drastic, different, and designed to grant everyone involved time, attention, and real relief for an extended period. It only makes sense. Taken in the proper light, a ninety-day stay can be seen for what it is—a bare beginning and a minimum for any serious intention.

Inpatient programs make the most sense. Indeed they are the most effective when your lost one is involved with crack cocaine, heroin, injected drugs, crystal meth, OxyContin, Xanax, long-term drug habits, a long history of treatment and failure, lengthy alcohol addiction, eating disorders, long-term depression and other severe psychiatric breaks or diagnoses, suicidal ideation, gambling addiction, is violent, or refuses to accept or follow psychiatric or medical treatment designed to allow normal life.

The beauty and appeal of inpatient treatment is the opportunity for the lost one to be completely immersed in recovery. It is full-time intensive education and therapy. The lost one is surrounded by people who share and understand their problems. There is a lack of judgment and a release from shame and embarrassment at inpatient facilities. The family, as well, gets a big break from drama and tension. Time and distance are critical luxuries at this point. Inpatient treatment brings focus and discipline, routine and progress back into shattered lives.

Again, I must stress the need for research, comparison, and dialogue with all of the facilities that seem useful. Each facility will be glad to fax or send you a schedule and a program overview. You will soon know which choice makes the most sense for you. Research. Listen, learn, and think.

EVALUATING TREATMENT OPTIONS

The Internet can be a big help in exploring different treatment options. Google any phrase that best describes your goal—such as "affordable alcohol rehab"—and make a serious start at your research. Try contacting the appropriate national and state agencies and foundations listed in the Resources section of this book. Also try any of the following for information: parole and probation officers, mental health agencies, hospital admission directors, clergy, doctors, district attorneys, nursing homes, lawyers, judges, and anyone you know who has gotten a friend or relative help. Use any and every resource you can think of. Tell each person your story, briefly, and ask for direction. You may be surprised at how willing they are to take time and help.

Following are some questions that are useful for assessing different treatment facilities:

Is there a treatment center nearby or where you have a relationship? This may make the choice more feasible. Convenience may be a big factor for you. Close by may also mean less cost overall. A relationship at any of these facilities may also mean greater trust and more information for you.

If you are a devout Christian or Orthodox Jew, or have some other religious or spiritual conviction, feel free to first seek out those places that are specifically designed for your lost one's faith. By the same token, don't shy away from facilities that are based in a certain faith simply because your lost one is not part of that faith. Investigate, weigh your options, and choose the best for the needs of your lost one. Sometimes your choices are among several options, none of which is perfect. You may, after careful evaluation, have to hold your nose and choose the best of what is available.

Is the facility an advocate of twelve-step recovery? This is an important question when considering someone with an alcohol or substance abuse problem. My experience suggests this is your best approach. Nothing works better.

Do they have a detox component? If they do, the whole process may be less complicated and more affordable.

Are they a social or medical model? In psychiatric cases and online behaviors, the medical model is often best. For drug and alcohol addictions, the social model may be more effective. The difference is simply the presence of medical professionals and medical monitoring, whereas in social models the emphasis is on support, understanding, and peer interaction.

Do the guests attend meetings during their stay? It is useful if the lost one is introduced to the twelve-step program while in an environment they trust and understand.

Do they advocate abstinence from all mood- or mind-altering substances? Not everyone does. This is important.

Do they accept insurance? This may be a critical factor for you.

Is financial aid available or a payment plan? Is there a sliding-scale option? Scholarships? This could really help out. Do not be afraid to ask.

Does the program include a family-group component during the treatment phase? The family group is a big plus and may be the biggest difference between similar programs.

Do they offer special-needs services, for either the handicapped or those with other special needs? This may be important for your lost one.

Is there medical staff inhouse? If your lost one takes any crucial medication, you need to make sure there's a protocol in place.

What is the policy regarding leaving before completion? Is the payment prorated? Can I get a portion of the payment back if they leave? This is good to know. What is their policy?

Do they have an aftercare program? This could also be a determining factor in similarly priced programs.

Is the facility co-ed? I prefer a gender specific track. Men meeting with men, women with women.

What is the ratio of staff to guests? Smaller is better.

Will they forward literature and a schedule to you? If not, move on.

Are they willing to share referral information with you? Again, why not? What are they hiding?

Are any staff members certified as drug and alcohol counselors? This is important. A lot is at stake—money, time, and the future. Find the best-qualified facility you can.

Are any of the staff in recovery? A useful bit of knowledge. I would prefer that someone be familiar with the actual dynamics of personal recovery.

Is there a psychiatrist or psychologist involved in the treatment regimen or affiliated with the facility? Always a good sign of how serious and effective they are.

Is there anyone currently enrolled who is of similar age or background to your lost one? Not critical, just helpful.

In addition to getting answers to the questions above, make sure to write down the following about each facility you contact:

- facility name
- address
- Web site

- phone number
- contact person
- when you spoke
- cost
- length of stay
- beds available starting when
- check-in time
- what can be brought in; what is restricted

This process is an excellent way of evaluating treatment options and gaining some clarity. Repeat it with several facilities and then begin to make your decision.

DEALING WITH THE COST OF TREATMENT

Now comes the big bugaboo: money. I hear from people near and far shocked by the cost of treatment. Here is a rough rule of thumb: inpatient psychiatric care, including treatment of eating disorders, can run around $1,000 dollars a day. Addiction treatment ranges from $100 a day at the low end to $1,000 or more at the high end. Why this is so is the topic of another book, one that needs to be written, but has not been.

More expensive does not mean better in treatment options; nor is the cheapest option always the best. For now I want to tell you that whatever strategy seems to fit your situation is the best one. Getting your lost one some help, granting you and your family some short-term relief, and having time and resources to plan the next move is the most valuable action you can take now. Decide what kind of program works best for you and the substances or behaviors involved, how long the optimal term of treatment is, and begin the research we have outlined above. The help is out there, and there is a way to make this work.

INSURANCE AND THE LOST ONE'S JOB

One of the main factors in successful intervention on an adult is addressing of the principal objections of your lost one before ever broaching the subject. Let's start with the job.

If your lost one is well liked and doing well at their work, you don't want to do any harm there. You need to research the human resource policies in place in your state and at the workplace. Will a trip to rehab cost them their job? Employers have been through a revolution in the last decade, becoming more aware of treatment and the benefits of supporting an employee who wants help. This does not mean they are gung-ho every time; nor does it mean they will understand and be helpful in your case. The factors seem to be these: How long is the employment history, how good an employee has the lost one been, what shape is the company in, how aware are they of the problem with your lost one, have there been warnings or disciplinary actions, how good is their insurance program, what is their policy regarding this issue? All of these issues have to be addressed discreetly. I cannot, in good conscience, tell you to start dialing the phone and announcing your great intentions to the HR department at your lost one's work or their insurance company or personal physician. I need you to think long and hard about a couple of basic questions: Do we use insurance at all? Are we ready to deal with the repercussions of whichever way we go? I believe these issues alone deter a huge number of efforts in this area. Money is the number two factor, after fear, that stops the process before it really starts.

So here are the steps to take, writing down the facts as they emerge. First, read the actual policy. If you can't find a copy, request one. If you cannot decipher the part that applies to treatment for addiction or psychiatric illness, ask for help. Ask anyone you know with a background in insurance, law, or contracts. Ask your pastor or simply call an insurance broker and ask for an appointment. Tell them you want to review your policy and that you need to understand the section on treatment before you decide to switch. Do not call the company and start naming names. You need to avoid all red flags, in case you decide on a different tack. Once you understand the policy, you can discuss it with the treatment center you choose to work with.

After you understand what your policy actually does, you need to think about the medical side of the equation. Treatment centers often need a medical clearance to admit someone without detox. They and you will also need a doctor's letter if you intend to use the insurance policy. Getting such a letter before the intervention is basically impossible. Your lost one's relationship with their doctor is confidential, and rightly so. Getting a physician to write a letter recommending treatment, without apprising their client, is not likely to happen. So here it is: if you decide to use your policy, tell the treatment center well in advance, give them a number where they can reach you, or tell them not to call at all, that you will contact them, and let them begin to tell you how to proceed. They have done this before and know how to go forward in order to use your coverage to your best advantage. Your lost one may qualify for medical leave, personal time, or even vacation days. Let's get all the facts.

Please be aware that this use of the policy will be written down in black and white forever, in several places. It will be a part of your lost one's medical history, employee information, insurance history, and on record at the treatment facility. Is all that confidential? Yes. Is it information that is too easy to get and not well enough protected? Yes. None of this should matter too much in the face of your lost one's life peeling toward disaster, but it needs consideration and thought.

Next, you will need the facts regarding the law in your state. Most states have made it hard to fire someone for seeking help, but the letter of the law differs from place to place. You can start your search for the facts at the state labor Web site or get phone numbers and get your information the old-fashioned way, by talking to a human. Get names, and write down the dates of your conversations. Ask for any relevant papers or pamphlets (sent not to your home) so that you can add them to your file. If this all sounds overwhelming, take a moment to think about what you've been dealing with so far. This stuff is not that hard to navigate; it wants attention and writing down, that's all. Make the calls, weather the details and the personalities you have to deal with, and get the facts. Then you can think straight, with some knowledge, instead of feelings and worry.

If your lost one is working independently or with a close friend or longtime associate, chances are your situation is not a secret. You may be surprised by how welcome any action on your part is likely to be. Some of these problems may actually be easier to deal with than you think. Let's find out, quietly and surely.

THE COURTS

When the courts are involved, treatment is often an excellent sign to both prosecutor and judge that your lost one is serious about changing. While they may be understandably cynical at first, any demonstration by your lost one of effort and willingness, along with reports from the treatment center and counselor, will make a positive difference with the court. Court officers see a constant parade of lying, denying, blaming, and failure. Any new show is remarkable to them, and having any progress and news on your side is a good thing down the line. If successful, this effort may be the most important factor in your lost one's future. Judges rarely punishes clean, sober men and women who are active in recovery the same way they would failures and liars.

Always check and make sure that a lost one under arrest or indictment may leave the area to attend treatment. Most courts will allow this move. Always notify parole or probation officers, as well as the court, where your lost one is and what they are doing. Make sense?

⚜

By now—the end of this chapter, that is—you have moved toward a solution, based in action, that requires a lot of looking, listening, and learning. We've learned about about the substance or behavior involved. We began to investigate the options available to us, their cost, and the time and distance involved. We've formed some ideas about our responsibilities and the ongoing commitment that family recovery entails. Finally, we got to the nitty-gritty of cost and affordability.

I hope this represents a profound change from where you were just a short time ago. Facts and figures are important, and now you can make an informed plan. The time of our solution is drawing near. Feel good about all you've done and hopeful about what lies ahead. Action and a knowledge of the truth mean that nothing will be the same again. Onward!

4.

READY, SET, GO!

The Pre-Intervention Meeting

⚜

Okay, you have made a decision. Congratulations. Now you need to walk through the process of assembling, organizing, and staging an intervention. Again, we will concentrate on facts not feelings. I know this is scary, but this is when families and friends do their best work: in crisis. We will get organized, and then we will act. This will work, if you follow direction and stick to the plan! Here we go . . .

WHO TO INVITE TO THE INTERVENTION

In general, the question is: Who is willing, motivated, and available? Who knows of the problem? Whom do you trust? To whom will the lost one most likely listen?

The guidelines are: family members mature enough to participate and friends and loved ones who are concerned and not directly involved in the addiction. The lost one's lost cohorts are obviously not a good idea. Involving colleagues from work requires thought: Are they discreet? Do they have only the best interests of the lost one in mind? Clergy or a doctor who is interested and onboard with the goals involved may be a positive. In terms of others, like ex-spouses or estranged children, these must be considered on a case-by-case basis. Follow your gut and your instinct for these issues. Never involve anyone not in complete agreement about the severity of the problem or the consequences for failure. Never. Otherwise, begin the formation of the "coalition of the willing."

You'll need to know:

Who is willing to participate? Don't not force, coerce, or judge anyone who is afraid or in disagreement with us.

Do they understand and agree with the process? Not having everyone onboard with the process, its goal, and the method employed—consequences for refusal, immediate commitment— makes for a clusterbomb. You don't need opinion or doubt in the room anymore. That ship sailed a long time ago. Discussion, argument, waiting, and seeing—that's all over now. You are in or you are out it is that simple. It needs to be if you intend to have any chance of succeeding. No more waffling. Remember, there is no judgment or criticism of those who are uncomfortable or afraid, no coercion. There is simply no time left for anything but unity and action.

It is a bad idea to introduce any last-minute participants. Their uneducated ego generally makes for the unfortunate belief that their "special bond" with the lost one will carry the day. Too many times people believe that there is some magical appeal or logic that will turn the tide—there is not—if you will just give them some time alone with the lost one. These efforts may disrupt the momentum of the process, allow for more argument and bargaining on the part of the lost one, and, frankly, waste time!

Can somebody who drinks or uses be involved? Yes, provided they are not directly involved in the use and securing of the substance and are not currently in crisis themselves. This goes to credibility and focus.

What about people who have not been "in touch" lately? Absolutely fine, and this may in fact have a great impact on the lost one. Look how many people know about the problem and care enough to do this difficult thing. Look how far they came and the effort they made to be here today. This can be powerful.

What about children participating? On the subject of kids and the state of your marriage or relationship, time is your friend. I generally discourage young kids having any part in an intervention, but teens or older kids may want to be involved, and they may be a powerful addition. If they have direct experience or recent history in the fallout from your lost one's using or behavior and can be supportive of the process and its goal, they should be considered. No child should be involved in a process as highly emotional as this one. No child should be asked to keep secrets. Too much pressure, too much responsibility. There are too many adult issues involved, and the meeting itself may be unhinged by their presence. Children may write a letter to be read and may be brought in at the end of the process, if the lost one agrees to seek help. No one who agrees to go to treatment should have to go without time with their kids, as long as they have not abused or molested them.

❧ *Harriet's Story* ❧

I was contacted by a woman who wanted to plan an intervention for her daughter, Stephanie. Over several phone calls it became obvious that this would not be a traditional intervention. There were not really any candidates for participation. There were too many exes (stepfathers, husbands, lovers).

Over a period of months we talked, researched, and planned while Stephanie wandered the streets high on crack and in danger. We all prayed that either the police or an ER visit might prompt a phone call.

One morning Harriet got the call: Stephanie had been ringing doorbells up and down the street, channeling messages from outer space through her fillings. Eventually one of the homeowners called the police.

This was our break: we swept into action. Because of all our preparation and planning and Harriet's hard work, we were ready. Stephanie was experiencing a psychotic break from her constant crack smoking, and she was placed under a seventy-two-hour psychiatric hold.

Harriet managed to extend this hold, since she had prepared for just such a chance! She managed to coordinate the staff of the facility her daughter was held in, the court that held jurisdiction, and the social services involved. After several months of detox and psychiatric treatment, we had a new Stephanie on our hands. She was released to her mother and entered a ninety-day program for women. She completed her treatment beautifully. Stephanie entered sober living and wound up staying for a year. I am pleased to say that she is several years sober, a woman of purpose and energy.

All of this is because of Harriet's tireless efforts and diligent planning. She never took no for an answer. Get ready, people.

THE PRE-INTERVENTION MEETING

Once you've decided who is in, you'll need to get together. And believe it or not, this can be a festive occasion. There is reason to feel good and excited. I know some of you will be scared. That's okay. Let's get to work.

First, pick a place where you have time and some space to gather. You can eat while you're at it if you want. Grandma can bring a covered dish if she feels like it. (This is not, however, an occasion for cocktails.) Try to sit down in a circle, so everybody can see one another. Begin by sharing the reason you are all together and how you each feel. This is good because so much of your life has been about the lost one for so long, and so much of it bad—but not anymore. How do you feel? What are you afraid of? What are your hopes?

Next, let's catch up on who knows what. Share any secrets or information that is new or important. You all need to understand, as much as possible, what is going on day to day with the lost one. We're only as sick as our secrets. We are not just having an intervention on the lost one you know, we are having an intervention on our system, our feelings, and our fears. Once you have gotten all that out on the table, each person's role will become clearer. One person may be able to recount things of which the others had no knowledge. Decide who will follow the lost one if they bolt, who will pack their bags, who will accompany them to treatment, who will bring the dip.

Choosing a Leader

Every group needs a leader. Who is yours going to be? Mom or Wife may not be the best choice, but "whatever it takes" is our new creed. Generally, the most interested or affected party has the most leverage. What works best, given the choices? Is there one among you whom the lost one has special regard for, whom they respect? Is there a special relationship between them and any of you? There is no wrong choice, as long as whoever is chosen understands the process and its goals and is willing and able. Often the person doing the research is the logical choice to organize and mobilize but not to actually lead the intervention in the room. It is up to you.

Let's call the person we select our "guide" or our "captain," or just our "fearless leader." Whatever you call them, you need one. Here's why: someone needs to be thinking through the entire deal, "what next." So much is happening in the room that a cool head needs to be dedicated to sticking with the plan. Where are we sitting? Who reads first, next? Who is our chase person if the lost one bolts? How do we begin? All of this cries out for order and leadership.

Select the person you all decide is best suited, and stick together behind them. Whoever it is, work through the plan with them, and use your pre-intervention meeting to see that all is in readiness.

Choosing a Location

The element of surprise is your biggest advantage. Decide now where the intervention will be held. You are looking for privacy, room, and time. Avoid the lost one's home or office, since we want control of the day. The reason we only want to use the lost one's space as a last resort is plain: they are likely to have drugs, alcohol, or other things available to them quickly and easily—or worse, have guns or other people present. Restaurants and public spaces like parks are not good. A hotel is okay or someone else's home or private office. Anyplace that you have access to and that works for you. My experience is that a neutral site is best, but anywhere can work.

How to Get Them There

You next need to decide how you are going to guarantee that the lost one shows up at a particular place and time on the day in question. If anyone wants to feel bad about the need to deceive the lost one in order to get them in place—oh well. How have they been treating you and the other people involved? Honestly, with respect and concern? Why has the lost one been hiding and lying about their behavior? How else can we proceed? To fool someone in order to save them seems to me a fair karmic deal. If this is the worst thing any of you have ever done, for any good reason, then congratulations—get over it.

The important thing is deciding what will guarantee the lost one's attendance. Who can carry that off? Good, they get the job.

When to Stage the Intervention

Next is deciding when the event can take place.

You need to think about the right time to move. Stay away from anniversaries, birthdays, major holidays, and divorce proceedings. One "big day" is enough in any week, so plan accordingly. We want to do this at a time of day that allows us to reach treatment immediately or to begin the journey so that we arrive during business hours. If this is impossible, arrange with the treatment center for after-hours' admission. Obviously this needs to be settled, in cooperation with the facility, ahead of time.

Then remember this: get there early and prepare. Assume the lost one will be late but pretend they will be on time. Be prepared to wait. Hide your cars whenever possible and consider meeting at another spot and sharing a ride to the location. Remember to sit in a circle when possible, and place the lost one closest to whomever they feel safest with. This should be easy to determine; of all involved, whom does the lost one feel the most fondness or trust for?

The Treatment Choice

At our pre-intervention meeting you will want to pass out any information, pamphlets, or literature you have regarding the treatment option you have chosen, as well as your intervention statements. Give everyone the Web site information if there is any, so that they can visit it at their leisure. Make sure everyone has everyone else's phone number, as well as the number and address of the treatment facility. Explain what you have learned about the addiction or condition involved and its treatment. Describe the place you chose and why. Talk about cost and length of stay. Go through the routine that the lost one will be following and mention any visiting or communication rules.

Who Does What When?

Decide on the order in which you will speak. There are no rigid guidelines here. Merely talk it through and decide. Generally, we want the person who is closest to the lost one to pose the final question—after the last statement has been read. This person will ask the big question, "Will you accept the help we are offering here today?"

The leader welcomes the lost one and explains briefly that people who love them are present to share with them and offer help. Will they sit down and listen? Everyone speaks in turn, directly from their statements, and everyone finishes. No argument, no defending, no explaining.

Go around the room, each person in turn reading the first statement only. When everyone has read that statement, begin again, going around the room in the same order, everyone in turn reading the second statement. Then, go around the room a final time, everyone reading the third statement. When the last person has read their third statement, they ask the big question.

The lost one may speak when all are done. Keep reminding them of the agreement, and tell them everyone wants to hear from them and they will get their turn. Be brisk, be firm, and be sure. Oh, and be ready for anything, including a miracle!

The Intervention Statements

At the pre-intervention meeting, you'll need to hand out the statement forms. I suggest writing or typing out the statements starting on page 99 and distributing photocopies. Discuss how they are used, the order they come in, and how to complete them. The first two statements concern how each person has seen addiction affect the life of the lost one and how their own lives have been affected. The third deals with the consequences of the lost one refusing treatment.

Let each person participating in the intervention get the anger and resentment out of their system now; it will be counterproductive on the big day.

Keep each statement in the "I" mode. You don't want to talk about secondhand information or things you heard. Speak from experience and personal feelings. *I* have seen this, *I* have been affected, *I* believe, *I* can or cannot, etc. Now is also a good time to tell the lost one about how they have changed: physically, emotionally, personality, habits, anything the participants have personally observed in the lost one.

Do not judge or blame. You do not need to shout, curse, or threaten.

These statements are scripted because it is important to be consistent and brief. And no, you may not "just wing it" when it comes to the written letters. No, you may not attend but not participate. No, you may not have one person read everyone's letters. This is not interpretive drama; this is a life on the line. The only person who may have a letter read for them is someone separated by illness, age, or continents.

It is important to start each statement with a positive comment or memory. "You know I love you" or "I've always cared about you" is fine. If the lost one has ever been of service to you, helped you out in a difficult time, or if the writer can site a specific time or place when the lost one was helpful or important to solving a problem or crisis, this should be noted and relayed to them. It will heighten their esteem, remind them of your regard for them, and let them feel how much a part of you they are.

Remember: it is important to always use "I" statements. "I have seen," "I have been affected," "I hope," etc. This keep things personal and fact-based.

Statement One: I *have seen your* _____ *affect* **your** *life negatively in the following ways:*

It is a good idea to talk about each substance or behavior involved, if there are more than one. Use specific incidents and observations, as recent as possible. Pull no punches. Wives or lovers should not, however, share details from their sex lives. In general, give the most powerful examples you can and talk about how you have seen them being affected, how you personally have been affected, and what you are most scared by. Do not be afraid to be emotional and frank. This may be your only chance. Always recall who they were before they were lost, and what you loved and miss most about them.

Statement Two: Your _____ *has impacted* **my** *life negatively in these ways:*

Again, be specific and brutally honest. Are the lost ones children, or are your own children or grandchildren involved? How has your trust been breached? Your own marriage, job, finances—have these factors been impacted? Think this over. Discuss it with those closest to you, and do some purposeful reflecting. This is a huge part of the process. Each comment matters.

A successful intervention must have a component of *leverage* or *consequence*. No family or group can recover in the face of refusal on the part of the lost one—or aid the recovery of the lost one—if they respond in the same way as they did previously. If nothing changes, nothing changes. Each participant must state clearly what the impact of refusal will be on their personal relationship with the lost one.

Statement Three: *It is not all right for me to continue to enable you to live like this as a part of our relationship. I can only support your life, and be a part of it,* **if you are willing to help yourself today.** *If you are not willing to take part in this recovery process* **today,** *you need to know that there will be consequences for your decision. Our relationship will change in the following ways:*

The Big Deal: Consequences

Consequences are at the heart of your intervention's success. Without resolve and agreement, you have no real leverage—and no real hope of success.

Each member of the group or family has to be willing to discuss how they have been manipulated by the lost one in the past for help, money, lies, secrets, favors, housing, cars, medicine, jobs— whatever the case is. Is enough finally enough?

No one must state a consequence, announce its timing, and then fail to follow through immediately! To do so is doom and failure! Is that straightforward enough for you? Forget even trying to intervene if you cannot identify and eliminate, completely, the ways in which you have each made the lost one's problem more manageable and less critical. If you cannot do this, you have no leverage and no shot. None.

At the pre-intervention meeting, talk about the possible consequences, argue among yourselves, always with one thing in mind: Can I really do this? I'm talking about not carrying them on your insurance or making car payments so the car isn't taken, not covering for them while they endanger other people, not allowing them around kids or grandkids with drugs or while actively sick or drunk. I mean stopping all payments, loans, paying for doctors, or anything at all, **for good.** Why are you doing it? Who is being helped? I am referring to allowing the lost one to drive without insurance, giving them a ride, allowing them to sleep in the garage or tool around with no license.

How long are you going to wait to do one right thing? Think, discuss, and decide. Make the consequences real, make them immediate, and make them sting. Is this hard to do? Yes. Is it the only rational response to insanity? Yes. Remember: the best definition of insanity is doing the same thing over and over again while expecting different results!

When you are through discussing the tone and content of each letter, especially the consequences, make sure you are all on the same page. Anyone who is uneasy is free to not participate, with no judgment and no hassle. Each person then takes the statements home and fills them in. This is crucial. These statements—including the consequences—are going to accompany them to treatment.

Remember: read the statement. Do not improvise! There can be no winging it. The leader needs to remind each person to bring their statement with them on the big day. Don't collaborate too much on these statements. They are personal and one-on-one. The lost one sees, hears, and feels each of them.

Details, Details

I know that where people sit, the order they read in, following the format, not arguing or defending, using "I" statements—all of this seems a little rigid and silly. I get it. I'm telling you now that the reasons this works are organization, the people, and the statements. There is a reason why you have not tried this before. You don't know how and it scares you. I do know how, and I'm not scared. I'm certain that sticking to the plan works and I'm equally convinced that trying it your way does not.

Remember the big question and how it is phrased: Will you accept the help offered to you today? The point is that all you have done, and all that will happen from here, is predicated on this question. It is provocative and important. Look them in the eye, reach for them, whatever you feel, and ask them sincerely. Then wait. Keep on point and focused. Order and direction matter. Either do this the way that works, or don't do it at all.

The Lost One's Objections

One of the big jobs you have undertaken is responding to each of the lost one's objections. I have asked you to go through all this trouble so that you can hope to never have to go through this much trouble ever again. I know this is difficult, but it's not as difficult as burying someone.

So here are typical objections from the lost one: I cannot leave work. I cannot leave my pet. I cannot leave my kids. I cannot miss the wedding, funeral, birthday, vacation, class, whatever. I cannot afford this. We cannot afford this. I can go later. I can do this on my own, especially now that I know how everyone feels. I am sick. I am hooked. I am scared. I cannot travel. I can't stand being around those people. I can't go to one of those places. It's too far, too dirty, too small. I need my own room. I need a doctor.

You must all be prepared for each objection, prepared enough to say, "It's taken care of"—whether it is or not. This means you have to look into financial, medical, legal, and professional matters and work it out. You need to think ahead for every possible complication and decide what can be done, temporarily, to make this work. Find the answers or make them up, but have answers that help you move the lost one forward. The lost one is a master of postponement and manipulation. Any doubts or hesitation will grant them the opening they need to divide and conquer. Be ready.

If They Run

Never try to block the lost one from leaving the intervention or the treatment center. Simply make sure you don't give them housing or help if they leave.

If they are determined to leave the intervention, let them. But first have the designated chasers tell them, even if they have to follow them to do it, that the meeting will continue and that their leaving will trigger a list of consequences. If the lost one asks "Like what?," the leader replies with the list of consequences and says that everyone in the room has agreed that they begin immediately. Then announce that you have a lot of work to do and phone calls to make and say good-bye, calmly. These are not threats, they are the responsibility of the lost one, whose behavior has caused them.

You also need to know how to respond if they leave the intervention and stay away for any real time. When they do call—and they will—you have only one answer to the call, no matter what they threaten or promise: "Only call me to say one thing, I'm ready to get help now! Any other conversation I'm not interested in. Enough is enough. Good luck. Good-bye."

If They Leave Treatment Early

You all need to talk about what to say when the lost one calls from treatment and announces they are leaving for whatever reason they think will fly. The facility is no good; they're out to get them; the people are all sicker than they are; they have learned all they need to know; they don't feel well; they miss the kids—whatever hokum they can cook up to get their way.

You all need to agree to respond in the same way: "I'm sorry you need to leave. I can't help you. I'll be sure to call everyone who cared enough to help and let them know what you have decided to do. I cannot aid you any longer in this destruction. I don't know where you will live but not here." Have the treatment center read the list of consequences to them before they leave. Call in if you can, on a phone conference, and reiterate that they have to face the consequences of their actions and decisions starting here and now!

PREPARING FOR THE LOST ONE'S TIME AWAY

Get a phone card or two if the treatment center is far away. They may not have phone privileges day and night, but often there will be a pay phone or a phone schedule.

Put someone in charge of packing a bag with travel stuff: deodorant, toothpaste, new toothbrush, aftershave, whatever the lost one may need to be away awhile. Know something about the routine where the lost one is going so that their clothes are appropriate. No shirts glorifying alcohol or drugs. No short skirts or Victoria's Secret wear. You can always send stuff that was forgotten or is needed later.

Find out exactly what they will need, and what is allowed in terms of phones, video games, CD players, iPods and books. Most places want none of this around to distract from the treatment process, so find out and honor those wishes.

It is all right to send a small amount of pocket money if the facility allows it, or you may wait and put money on their books. Know the rules of the treatment center and follow them. Fax the insurance card when asked, and have the lost one take a photo ID.

Also, it is always good to pack family or children's photos for the lost one to take along.

At the pre-intervention meeting you will also need to decide how you are going to handle their kids, pets, bills, and other responsibilities while they are away.

⚘

Finally, in planning your intervention, be aware that all of these objections we are addressing, all of the reasons not to go forward are part of the feelings that have been scaring you away in the first place. Your lost one counts on all of this keeping everyone away. Most of all they count on your fear. Please get out of the mind-reading business. I get that no one knows the lost one better than you, and I get that you are the one living with the problem. Now *you* need to get a couple of things straight in *your* mind. Your job is deciding what is and is not okay with you. Your job is deciding when enough really is enough. Your job is what you are doing, for your kids, your family, and your future. From the time you picked up this book, the present changed from another day of fear and feeling helpless to a day of action based in fact. There is power here and peace to be had in this knowledge: you are taking action, and there will be results. Believe this: something is going to happen, and nothing will be the same afterward. What are you more afraid of—the future with action or the future without it?

Be ready, be determined, and be sure that what you are doing is vital for life and love to thrive. Be strong and have hope. Someone has to, and it has to be soon.

5.

SURPRISE!

Intervention Day

❧

We are planning a surprise party unlike any other, counting on the shock value of putting a number of people from the lost one's life in front of them, all of whom are going to speak honestly and openly to the lost one on a very painful, scary subject: their loss of control, how it has affected them, and what they are prepared to do to help. More important, you are each going to describe to the lost one how life will change for them and for you if they do not accept the help you are offering.

Finally, the lost one will hear from you in a safe, controlled environment, where you have the support of others who share your concern. You will be able to deal in facts and feelings and to offer them a solution with a real end in sight. The fact that you have decided enough really is enough will introduce a new element into your discussion: the real bottom line!

When a group discusses and decides something, it has more

power. It is easier for a group to confront and control. There is power in numbers. For once you have things on your side: you picked the time and place and you decided what would work for you and yours—not the other way around, with you insanely dancing to a tune played by a sick person.

The next big element of success for us in our undertaking is time: the lost one hasn't got much of it left, and they are about to find that out. They don't know it, but you messed around and wound the clock. It's ticking, and for once you decided what time it really was. Time for a change. Not tomorrow or next week, or after the Super Bowl or after anything—*now*.

Preparation is the other big key. You have that going for you now, too, in spades. You have become an expert on your lost one's condition and its treatment. You are in possession of the facts—where the lost one can get help, when they can go, what it costs, how all the other issues in their crazy life can be addressed—all to allow some resolution to what seemed impossible only days ago. Now we get to rally our coalition of the concerned, the posse of love, or whatever you decide to call yourselves. The point is you are in the final phase, preparing to launch.

LOOKING BACK

This is a good time to look back and remind ourselves what we are fighting and what we are fighting for. I want to tell you a little about miracles first. I do not pray for miracles; I work for them. I don't hope for miracles; I expect them. I have been in the room when many occurred.

They all had different stories, different drugs and problems, and were different ages. Eventually they got lost. They each wound up in a room with me. I got to be a part of their recovery and to make them a part of mine. I remember every one of them. I remember the miracles so that I can face the sadness of the lost ones who were never found.

The radical action and the simple sense at the core of what I do, and how I do it, can seem cold or unforgiving, but the truth is that what you and I are planning is the most forgiving effort there could ever be. Remember: intervention is a profound act of love and hope in action.

Now is the time to expect your miracle. Nothing too dramatic, just a period of decision making and relief, while everybody gets a chance to start fresh and try again to help one another. My work and experience and your applied energy can yield the time that we need, and more. To manage to stop addiction and its destruction, to halt unchecked mental illness, to install a system of effective family responses to crisis—these are all formidable goals. To do so while also gaining mental health and some spiritual relief, well, I call it miraculous.

Once the lost one is found, the rest of your family can turn more of their attention back to their own lives and one another. This phase of recovery is precious: time to feel the relief and then move toward a deeper understanding, preparing for the return of your lost one to everyday life. The next phase is even better: reunion and time to just do normal things in a normal way. The luxury of moments and days when you all can simply be together without anxiety and crisis will hold a sweetness for you. I promise.

Whatever has taken them away from you—alcohol, drugs, porn, mental illness, gambling—no matter what happened to them, they have something in their life that has them so ensnared so that they can no longer choose you and your life together as the most important commitment. Their main job has become getting the time and opportunity to do something else, something so demanding that they will lie, cheat, steal, lose you and their job, kids, reputation, anything just to have their "magical medicine," their "relief." You probably will never know what that means, what it feels like. I hope you never do. You will never understand what has happened to you or them. It mostly has nothing to do with you. That is hard for most people to accept, impossible for some. The lost one wants something so badly, all the while knowing it is destroying them. Conflict, secrecy, and extreme selfishness have gained the upper hand in their lives, and yours has been changed forever as well.

Recovery from addiction and managing life with mental illness are long-term, learned commitments. For the lost one, being parted from their obsession is a terrifying prospect. Your lost one is about to be reduced to having to choose what matters most in front of all of you who cared enough to intervene.

Now we need that last element, a real empathy and a certain humility in the face of our task. We may always have been sympathetic, feeling moved to try to help the lost one. Here I am talking about empathizing with the truth of their own lonely struggle. They have withdrawn from life. They have surrendered their minds and spirits to something dark and deadly. We need to contemplate for a moment what that must be like.

Whatever pain you have felt, however you have dealt with loss and tragedy before, remember what you felt at your lowest point. Now assume for a moment that your lost one goes to bed at night (if they go to bed at all) and awakens with that same dread certainty in their heart and mind every single day. They face knowing this day will be as black as the last one, focused on getting and concealing their fix: hiding, planning, lying, and spiraling further away every hour: away from the people who love them, away from the chance for help. That is not living—it is waiting to die.

Each day they are a little (or a lot) sicker and less able to speak any truth. They have grown incapable of any meaningful human relationships. Think about that, and what it did to you and all of the people who want to help. Now contemplate how long they have been falling through space, alone. Their landing day is near, thanks to you and the love you are showing, and all the people who have come together. How great is this? Be grateful and full of a humble thankfulness. Finally, something is going to happen, something positive and out in the open.

This is a special time for you. You have worked very hard, very quickly, to get up to speed and figure out the truth of your situation. Now you are about to face the lost one in a new way. They are in there, hiding. Unless they are damaged in some profound way, they can be redeemed and renewed given time and help. You are bringing an answer, humbly and hopefully.

There is no more time for accusations, anger, recrimination, resentment—all the things you have a perfect right to feel. You are armed with facts, arrangements, and requirements. You have everything you need to help them get back to square one and make another start. Never forget why you are here.

No matter what happens, you and your family will not have to deal with the lost one's problem in the same way ever again. The family will not be doing business in the same way ever again. You and yours will not settle for a seat at the sidelines to watch the funeral ever again. You will not finance or lie for the lost one ever again. You will never be able to pretend or ignore again—ever. Not if you have decided enough is enough.

It's time for that miracle.

THE INTERVENTION

An intervention is an unusual gathering. There is no other event quite like it. Everyone involved is under pressure. Usually the tension and the fear are factors that have been present for a long time, building and taking on power. Some of you are scared, all of you are feeling anticipation and a mixture of hope and dread.

For the lost one, a whole bunch of feelings are about to be stirred up: fear, anger, resentment, shame, guilt, embarrassment, and worry that their magical friend is about to be ripped away from them on very short notice. They are shocked that the silence is being broken. You are about to break a lot of what I like to refer to as the unspoken rules of sick families. The hostages are all out of the trunk with the tape off their mouths, roaming around free. They are talking to each other and telling the truth out loud. "Dive, dive," screams the lost one's mind. They are panicked, as well they should be. They must either flee, hoping to turn on the drama/chaos switch that has served them so well in the past or stay and fight.

They need to see you and the group in a tailspin of argument, bargaining, and pointless division. They must pull out all the stops, using their powers of manipulation, denial, and distraction to try to divide or distract this scary bunch one more time from their mission. They need time to think, plan, regroup, and get their sick way: to continue to fail while holding all of you hostage.

Preparation is key. Our ducks can't just be in a row; they need to be in tight combat formation. Every detail concerning our plan has to be double-checked, verified, and listed at our pre-intervention meeting, then recapped right before we begin. You and your group must be a united team with an answer for every objection and solutions for each real problem posed. By the time you are ready to walk into the room and start your intervention, there are no more mysteries, no questions still hanging in the air except one: are you going to accept the help we offer you today?

On the day of the intervention, we need to meet briefly at a place of our choosing—a restaurant, a park, a home, a hotel room, our church, or wherever we decide—and do a final check of our preparations. Advance preparation and an understanding of what we are about are the most crucial factors in the success of our effort. It is easy to overlook one or several of the endless list of details or reminders. Review is prudent and reassuring. Here is a checklist that will help you keep track of the details, small and large, that add up to a smooth, effective intervention effort.

INTERVENTION CHECKLIST
- Where is the lost one?
- Where is the lost one's photo ID?
- Are their bags packed?
- Are there medications that need to be taken to treatment? (Put all bottles in one bag.)
- Who is in charge of rounding up all the prescription medications our lost one is using?
- Did we remember to get a new toothbrush, toothpaste, deodorant, etc.?

- Do we have a phone card? (No cells, so have the lost one write important numbers down.)
- Do we have stamps, envelopes, and a notebook (handy for the lost one for notes, suggestions, etc. while at treatment)?
- Did we pack family photos for the lost one to take along?
- Does the lost one need cigarettes at the facility?
- How much cash is allowed at the facility? Do they need money? Reminder: don't give the lost one any significant amount of money. Ten bucks ought to do it.
- Where is the contact number and information, such as visiting hours, directions, and rules, of the treatment facility?
- Who has the payment?
- Is there an insurance or prescription card?
- Where are the plane tickets or other travel documents?
- Do we need a hotel at our destination?
- Is everybody here?
- What order will we be speaking in?
- Who is our leader?
- Who will speak last and formally pose the big question?
- Who is our chase person?
- Who is escorting the lost one?
- When should we leave in order to make it on time? Remember, no delay in going to treatment. Kids, pets, Grandma—all should be handy and get a chance to say good-bye afterward. The longer you wait, the more time there is for something to go wrong—and it will. They will change their minds, or, worse, weaken your resolve.

In the Room

By now you have a leader who will welcome the lost one into the room; you know the order in which you'll be speaking; you know who will be speaking last and posing the big question.

The lost one sits and listens to everyone as they take their turn and responds only after all have spoken. If they refuse, they must leave. If they decide to leave, you must tell them of the changes their refusal will trigger—immediately. Whether they stay and listen or not, the list will be read.

Everything changes today, starting with how you behave as a group. Respect one another, support one another, and love one another. Most of all stick together.

The lost one is allowed to feel whatever they feel. But they are not allowed to offend or threaten violence. They are not allowed to abuse anyone verbally. They are not allowed to jump up, rush people, scream and shout, run out of the room and back in, interrupting people or arguing. You and your leader need to be clear with everybody in the room: these behaviors will be dealt with quickly and decisively.

They are allowed to leave. Never try to physically restrain anyone from leaving. You have no such rights unless the lost one is a minor. Only the chasers chase; no one screams back; all remain calm and determined. Let them make their display, then continue, always asking if they are willing to listen. Assure them that you will listen when you are done.

If they wish to stay, fine. If not, they are free to flee. But believe me, if you follow the plan and advise the lost one of what lies ahead after they leave, the consequences and actions you all are going to take, no matter what, it is a remarkably effective tool. Calm determination will freak them out! Mean it, do it, and watch what happens.

Never wait more than a couple of hours if the lost one does run away. Simply finish your business, decide when you will all speak again, and go about the business of implementing the consequences.

There is no such thing as a failed intervention if these rules are followed.

❧ *Jeremy's Story* ❧

It is so important to prepare for the unexpected when you begin your intervention plans: anything can happen.

I got a call from a family. Their son was in crisis. They believed he was using drugs and knew he was on the street.

In the process of adjusting to all the factors and figuring out how to make the intervention work, we were faced with getting everyone to LA, meeting and planning the intervention, where to take him to treatment, how to pay for it, and, most important, how to get the lost one to a site where we could stage the event.

A woman that knew the family and was the lost one's godmother felt sure she could get him to her house, and since they had enjoyed a close relationship, we agreed. The woman could not attend the pre-intervention meeting, and we soon discovered that she was not willing to believe that her godson was using drugs or addicted.

It became plain that she was convinced that her love and understanding could save him. To her, this was not a team effort but a challenge. The day slowly unraveled and it became apparent that at each important crossroad she would undermine the unity of our effort by bargaining and digressing. The final straw was her insistence on being left alone with him. In that meeting she began to make a deal with him, promising him rewards and help.

The young man decided that he did not need to listen to his family and refused their help. As he defiantly drove off in his truck (the one the family was paying for) everyone was devastated. To them, Jeremy seemed truly lost. The mother eyed the new duffel bag she had packed for her son's trip to rehab, filled with new clothes, shampoo, stamps, and some family photos. She cried as she threw it back into the trunk of her car. We assured them that this was not over. As I've learned over the years, there is no such thing as a failed intervention.

(Continued on page 137)

SURPRISES

When a surprise is revealed, or secrets are revealed that are deeper and more devastating than anyone could have imagined (suicide attempts, sexual or physical abuse, molestation, terminal illness), the leader must call it to the attention of the group, propose that this new information needs to be confirmed and dealt with at another time and place, while stressing that this is even more reason to proceed to treatment.

You must never try to deal with several interrelated issues at once. We are not here to resolve an ugly divorce, deal with adultery, or solve financial problems. There is only one issue before the group: the lost one is either going away today or they are not, period. Do not cease the process for any reason other than threats of suicide or violence. In those cases, summon the police. Take this seriously. Everything else can be sorted out in the wake of the intervention. This will be easier and better for the group, since they are already united.

Confirmation of explosive accusations needs to be thorough and painstaking. Start with the time, place, and nature of the events stated, and seek evidence, testimony, and professional guidance, either from law-enforcement authorities, social services, a private investigator, or using whoever or whatever you feel is most effective. Obviously this needs to be handled case-by-case.

No intervention can ever proceed when threats of suicide or violence are made. Emergency help must be summoned on the spot, with all witnesses remaining at the location until the responders arrive and take complete statements.

BARGAINING

Any negotiation or modifying of consequences in order to entice agreement is a waste of time. No bargaining! Once you step on the slippery slope of compromise, you are undone. Never forget that.

The number one crime of all intervention groups is the failure to follow through with meaningful consequences. If I could, I would have this tattooed on your forehead. Most family members with a lost one are incapable of rational thought and action where illness is involved. This is why we work as a group, not alone.

They don't get it, they never will, and they want to solve the problem quickly and quietly. This will never happen. If enough really is enough, act like it! Do everything differently than before. Start by meaning everything that you say.

You have to believe your family is more important than any one sick person. You have to believe that the way to mental health is through truth and action. You have to believe that you deserve relief and help. Most of all, you have to mean business. You and your family are about to disrupt a corrupt and useless emotional system, a model of dysfunction and adjustment that took years to solidify. Be bold. Refuse to accept and support the system that is killing your lost one and destroying your family.

Consequences, and your willingness to apply them, are your most powerful tool. Without this resolve, you are doomed. Don't even bother going through the motions—the whole ordeal is pointless. You better hear me now and believe me later.

ACCEPTANCE

Acceptance by the lost one may be spontaneous and immediate or a gradual, wearing-down sort of exercise. Either way, we all need to congratulate them, hug them, and laugh and cry together. Speak now of hope and love and how proud you are of them. Assure them again of your support and commitment. Talk about the future and the joy you all feel. Laugh about the tension and fear. Share your relief. This is a big deal!

Inform them of your research and what you know of where they are going. Tell them about visits and calls, and how you will all use the mail and the phone to communicate. Support and encourage. Never begin to rehash or recriminate! And remember that the statement of consequences accompanies them to treatment.

REFUSAL

I know that the refusal of a lost one is heartbreaking. I know the whole thing seems futile and hopeless. But you are wrong.

This effort by those who love and care for the lost one has given everyone a new and healthier perspective on the lost one's condition, on their role in the lost one's recovery, and on their own recovery. Everyone needs to move forward, dedicated to their own coping and future actions regarding the lost one.

You need to concentrate on the consequences of refusal now. These are the tools that will eventually leverage the lost one's acceptance of the reality of their situation and of the hopeless nature of their addiction or behavior. While the lost one has felt threatened, they have also had a tremendous wake-up call: the hostages are out of the trunk, they all know, and they are communicating with one another! This is huge. They have been insisting to themselves that they are not hurting anyone, and what they do is their business. Now they know better, and time is your ally. The lost one will often reconnoiter, begin to experience the consequences of their refusal, and suddenly have an epiphany: this won't fly anymore. Let it be their idea, that's fine. Support the decision, but act immediately. They may change their mind minutes later. Most important, continue on your path; hold firm and wait. Never give up hope. I know that in this sense, no intervention is really a failure!

GETTING TO TREATMENT

Remember, always, that there can be no delay in getting to treatment after acceptance of the plan by the lost one. It's really never a good idea to postpone or delay. Let the lost one visit with the kids, or say good-bye to the dog, or whatever needs doing, now. State the plan, execute it, and move on. If adjustments must be made, make them. If you absolutely must delay, detail someone to accompany the lost one while they wait.

Finally, whatever the outcome, let's celebrate our togetherness and our progress. Plan to revisit one another in the aftermath and to share feelings and thoughts with each other. This is your life, enjoy the time, and work together as much as you can.

6.

THE YOUNG AND
THE RESTLESS

Young People in Crisis

❧

The addiction epidemic is particularly troublesome when it comes to our children. Parents are busier than ever before and beset by increasing challenges from all sides: more costs associated with school and after-school activities, more independence at younger ages for kids, more to do and less time to do it all in. In the event that trouble begins at school or at home, the parent has to make a series of difficult decisions based on conflicting agendas. The desire to protect adolescents from consequences, the need to guide and support them toward the future while trying to understand their feelings and problems, and often getting the silent treatment from them, or worse, while in the middle of an unfolding drama—well, it can all be too much.

Helping to save a lost adolescent with an intervention requires a great deal of stamina and determination and may be one of the most emotional, transformative experiences of your life. Those who haven't already experienced it won't understand. The good news is that you've got more leverage and options than you are ever going to have, and now you are going about it in the best way possible.

YOUNG PEOPLE IN CRISIS

Sean and I must assume that if you are reading this deeply into our work, your adolescent is truly in crisis. We are not writing for the parent whose son or daughter went away to band camp and puked in their trombone one crazy night around the campfire. We're not writing for the woman whose nephew had one too many at his bar mitzvah and set the drapes on fire. There is, in my experience, a wide range of age-specific testing, acting out, and experimentation that is predictable, normal, and possibly even healthy. Our book is not for the parents of those young people. We must, from this point forward, assume that you have observed or been made aware of a pattern or history of dire failure, escalating consequences, and have enough evidence to be genuinely alarmed.

If this is the case, then I want to guide you now through the early, most confusing period of your journey, the *initial response period.*

If you are currently in crisis with a young person, you need to accept one idea wholeheartedly: this is war! To succeed in war, we need to pick our battles. This brings us to a discussion that needs to take place sooner rather than later. You will need for all involved to agree on the severity of the crisis and the responses you propose. Your child's property (their stuff), space, and deeds are now all subject to investigation and control. You must begin now to locate facts and social rituals that are an important part of your adolescent lost one's life. We need facts! Your home, energy, affection, and finances are all in play, and none of them are a given any longer. Critical issues of trust, love, and responsibility are in the balance. From MySpace to the cell phone, diaries to backpacks or purses, text messages to closets and cars—all must be searched and searched thoroughly and repeatedly.

I absolutely cannot tolerate all the pious discussions I hear from delusional parents that insist on the sanctity of their child's space or property. Sentences that start with "I would never dream of . . ." and end with *searching, eavesdropping, spying,* or *questioning* need to be repudiated here and now with this response: fine, start dreaming of the funeral or, if you're lucky, making time for jail visits. If this sounds shrill or extreme, so be it. How high are the stakes? I cannot tolerate the attitude "They are only ———." Fill in the blank: only smoking pot, only having unprotected sex, only slowly failing and dying? Are you a responsible party, bound to protect and nurture—or are you their buddy, their cool peer?

The adolescent lost one needs a loving and concerned parent, ready to do what is necessary. I am weary of listening to the reasons that parents use to justify doing none of the work before them, while attending the failure of their child. Either your trust and love have been violated or they have not. Either your child's life and future are in the balance or they are not. Which is it?

After years of work in the field, I believe the response progression is best characterized by the following phases: I believe my child is in crisis. I will confront the issue at the next opportunity, either poor grades, an arrest, a lie, an accident. Whatever the next incident is, it is the occasion for an agreement between the child and the guardian, parent or parents. The child participates in a document being drawn up, specifically addressing the unacceptable behavior. You can find a sample contract in the Appendix. Consequences are agreed upon. Whatever those consequences are, they must be immovable, nonnegotiable, hard and fast. Get it? These may range from loss of social time away from the home; forfeiture of cell phones, allowances, or jobs; to drug tests; withdrawal from extracurricular activities, and sports teams; or even removal from the school currently attended. The severity should be progressive, triggered by certain failures. Any adolescent in legitimate crisis will be unable to abide by such an agreement. The first failure we can write off to a normal instinct to test the boundary. Fine, then we invoke the consequence. Any failure to follow through on your part will spell your doom and your inability to see this thing through. Then you are beyond my help.

As I said, expect failure. You must test them for drugs and alcohol, at your discretion. You may purchase home test kits from the pharmacy or use the local hospital or clinic for a blood or urine test. Either way works. The only child who will refuse to be tested is one with no intention of honest effort. We're not going to indulge the child in crisis in some fuzzyheaded debate about civil rights or respect. That is all over now. They have already made clear by their behavior that questions of respect and responsibility are beyond their abilities. You gave them an arena to demonstrate their intentions, to earn back trust and respect, and they have failed to grasp the severity of the situation. That is your job. All testing should be random and unannounced in advance. Simply produce the kit, or take them to the location you have decided on and insist that no one is going anywhere until a sample is supplied.

Upon the occasion of the next failure, it is time to kick in the next phase of your agreement. They must be interrupted in their drinking or drug using. You will search for outpatient facilities in the area. Do they also have a participation track for the family? If not, search on. If there is no such facility anywhere nearby, what is the best of what is available? Ask to speak with parents who have sent their kid through the program. Don't let them tell you this is impossible because of confidentiality. Any father or mother or sister or brother who has seen a miracle of recovery through any program would gladly call and encourage another parent or guardian. The center can contact them and pass on your number.

We are of two minds on the subject of intensive outpatient treatment. Outpatient treatment, at its best, is a five-day-a-week meeting place, staffed by certified counselors, trained to deal with adolescents in crisis. The parents generally meet once or twice a week. After x number of days, weeks, or months, attendance requirements may be tapered, or simply end. By that time the child should grasp that this behavior simply will not wash.

Upon their completion of outpatient therapy, you must continue to track them, check up on their whereabouts—and test them, randomly and at your discretion. I understand this all sounds like a lot of work, mostly by you, for their problem. If they were dying of cancer, would you have similar complaints? You need to ask yourself, at each phase of this journey, is it worth it? I believe any responsible parent will do what it takes to find resolution and happiness for their child. If my child fails again, I must be prepared for radical action.

I believe that adolescent treatment is the hardest work in the field. We need to be honest with ourselves about our own habits now. Do we drink in our home? Is wine routine at dinner? Is liquor or champagne associated with celebration and holidays? All of this may have to be examined and altered in the short range. Did we drink and party when we were young? All of these factors matter. Also of interest is family history. Are there alcoholics in the family? The family needs to talk about all of this.

I feel it is inappropriate to drink or use drugs in front of any adolescent in crisis or recovery. If you must keep liquor in your home—I cannot imagine why that would be so important to any parent—lock the cabinet and mark the level of alcohol in the bottles. No friend or loved one should drink or use in front of, or around, an adolescent in recovery. Surely drinking with dinner can be suspended for a significant period of time, say six to twelve months. Unless you also have a drinking problem, not drinking for a while should not be a problem.

Here is the protocol I advocate for parents of both the adolescent in serious crisis and the adolescent with a long history of any of these problems. I want you to decide how much failure and heartache would help you decide to take the radical action I am suggesting: ninety days or more in an intense wilderness or inpatient program. Would overdose, a fatal accident, an arrest for felony charges be enough to convince you? How about my personal guarantee that your child's adult life would be compromised and plagued by mental health and addiction problems owing to your failure to act decisively in these years? Because that is what is at stake for you, in my experience, nine times out of ten, if you fail to take decisive action now.

Common sense says, and science confirms, that the longer we postpone the use of drugs, alcohol, and sexual activity, the healthier our children will be and the more apt they are to be mature in their decision making. I also know that the more swiftly we respond to crisis, and the better our preparation and research, the more likely we are to reclaim a lost child's life. Nothing could be more powerful and healing for a family.

Here are some special concerns and recommendations. First, take note of the status we have assigned the substances or behaviors involved in the previous pages. For all the 3-D notations, we have very specific recommendations that offer hope of real recovery. This often means interrupting school and leaving all other activities behind, lousing up holidays, vacations, or forfeiting prepaid fees or enrollments. I urge you to apply common sense amidst a minefield of contrary opinion and concerns.

To sum up, inpatient treatment is a logical step when outpatient treatment and local therapists have failed. In the face of repeated failure with contracts, outpatient therapies, and counselors, it is time to take more drastic measures. The environment and routine must be interrupted. You will also want to pay attention to your child's companions, their music choices, their art, and their general mood, speech, and sleep patterns. If a young person is suddenly into screeching death metal music, doodling pictures of sadomasochism and blood-covered virgins, all while locked in their room—something is rotten in Denmark.

TREATMENT OPTIONS FOR ADOLESCENTS

Among the fastest-growing segments in the treatment industry is treatment for adolescents. There are now a bewildering variety of treatments. So, it is important to look at the various options and their advantages and applications.

Wilderness Camps and Outdoor Programs

I am a believer in the power of change. I have seen the good that can come from taking an adolescent or young adult in turmoil out of the environment they are accustomed to and offering them challenges and support that allow a sense of self and self-worth to emerge through day-to-day outdoor adventure and individual counseling. Assessment and diagnosis can be greatly aided by the opportunity to interact with a young person who is free of many of the stressors present in their normal life.

I'm *not* writing about the so-called "boot camps" that are enjoying some popularity. I have no experience with them. I am skeptical about the value of the entire approach of such organizations, and I'm not comfortable encouraging parents to enroll a child in such programs.

I am speaking of certified programs, based in the twelve steps or similar spiritual tenets, staffed by mental health professionals and designed by licensed professionals. These are based on therapeutic models, designed by accredited psychiatric practitioners.

I am a big believer in these treatment options, particularly for kids showing the first signs of any crisis. Experience has taught me that a huge number of young people who are beginning to show signs of failure or negative behaviors that disrupt the home often need basic attention. Any young person who is unraveling, either with drugs or through destructive behaviors, needs a safe period of time away from everything and everybody.

Separation from peers and habits, routine and pressure, is an incredible relief. The suspension of the constant dialogue and familiar patterns of argument and worry is valuable as well. Most of all, the establishment of a structured, healthy outdoor alternative that is free from outside concerns and influences, in my experience, often results in the quickest and most valuable gains in self-esteem and outlook in the shortest time possible. The effect can be dramatic. I believe that the advantages of these programs lie in their simple emphasis and approach: they concentrate not on what is wrong with your child but identify and nurture what is right with them.

Wilderness programs are best when the young person in question has recently begun to spiral out of control. For boys or girls, particularly in the fourteen- to seventeen-year-old range, the luxury of escape from the unbelievable drama and constant judging and negativity that is high school can prove miraculous. There are also special programs for the challenging eighteen to twenty-four age range.

I know of cases in which parents have been stunned at the profound change precipitated by an outdoor program: a smiling, healthy kid, looking them in the eye and talking a blue streak! Priceless.

It is worth noting that many of these programs also provide a "house call" service, whereby they aid in the process of confronting and transporting the young lost one.

Sometimes the *"great answer"* is simply having time and space alone, surrounded by understanding. For the lucky parent who finds this solution early, congratulations. Please count your blessings and help get out the word. These programs are also good for adolescents who have formed intense romantic or obsessive relationships close to home. Often the chance for insight, exercise, laughs, adventure, independence, and growth will bring back what has gradually been eroded by the craziness of recent crisis.

A young person can gain a great deal of confidence when challenged by a new, positive group of influences and assurances. Especially in the case of girls, the benefits of physical challenge and consistent engagement in a positive, outward-focused life outdoors is almost gone from their experience. Few families can supply unhurried, extended vacations without distraction, under the guidance of professionals, while taking care of the rest of life—much less get their kids to actually talk to them, honestly, about what they are feeling.

The good outdoor programs offer an amazing opportunity for everyone involved to get a genuinely productive time-out, while letting the lost child experience something completely unique. I feel confident that a young person whose drinking and drugging activities have been interrupted early has the best chance of getting maximum benefit from this kind of program.

Wilderness programs are also effective for lots of things besides drug or alcohol addiction or abuse. There are wonderful programs for dual diagnosis, specialized educational needs, and a range of options from mild eating disorders to gender confusion. There are also effective programs for defiant teens, runaways, and kids who cannot seem to make it in normal school settings because of learning differences or behavioral issues.

I do not recommend wilderness programs for chronic eating disorders, of for those with severe mental illness, serious medical challenges, rage issues, or post-traumatic stress disorder. I also prefer programs that are not coed, but it's not a deal breaker.

I cannot emphasize enough how vital it is to investigate your choices thoroughly. The good programs encourage anyone interested to read testimonials posted on their Web site. But you need to go several steps further. Ask the program director for an interview, either by phone or, if practical, face-to-face. Request a tour, again, if it is practical. Ask the program director if you can be contacted directly by parents who have enrolled their child; tell the director to pass your number along. Research the staff members' accreditations and licensing, as well as the length of time the program has operated. Call the business bureau that applies to the area of operation and see what the history is. Also check with the relevant state division responsible for licensing the operation. An educational therapist in your area can be informative and helpful regarding nearby facilities. You can simply look up "educational therapists" online or in the phone book. And never apologize or feel that you are bothering anybody in the process. This may be the most important decision, to date, in your parenting life and for the future of your child. Be thorough and determined to get answers.

Outpatient Programs

These are a source of much discussion between Sean and me. We feel these programs have such a combination of weaknesses and promise that the whole subject can be frustrating.

For the treatment of adolescents, the advantages of outpatient programs are affordability, familiarity, insurance coverage, convenience, and participation by the family in the group sessions normally offered. The fact that we needn't disrupt school and other routines can also be appealing. I believe these programs are best used as a first response type of resort.

If you have already done an academic intervention—that is, if you've dealt with a sudden or gradual failure in grades and study, and then been faced with the addition of a drug or alcohol problem, outpatient treatment may be the proper option. As a way to fulfill probation requirements, either academic or legal, they are a good tool. They're also often used as a diversion program, allowing a teen with an arrest to avoid jail.

The big weakness of these programs is that, often, for the adolescent, nothing changes. Parents tend to think, "Well, things are happening; the problem is being handled by professionals." Unfortunately, at a local facility, the faces are familiar, the drill boring, the meetings crowded, and the staff overworked and underqualified. They lack drug-testing components and, frankly, are designed to get insurance companies off the hook quickly and cheaply. Meanwhile, the young person's secret life and environment remain undisturbed. My experience tells me that for more serious long-term addictions and problems, outpatient programs lack the necessary staff, skills, components, and intensity to accomplish anything besides marking time. They are often an incomplete answer.

Finally, I must point out that they are almost always coed. I cannot endorse the idea of taking a mixed bag of boys and girls with a gamut of problems of varying severity and length, having them meet after school in a socialized setting close to home, only to have them meet up again at the mall later. On its face the idea seems silly and potentially dangerous.

But, for most families, outpatient programs remain the number one option because of convenience, affordability, and a need to believe things are not that bad. I would insist that an outpatient program have a family group component. Without the family work being done as an adjunct to your lost one's therapy, you will be wasting your time and money. As we have said, the entire family has become bruised and a little dazed. You all need to be a part of something that has direction and a promise of progress. If this is the most practical, affordable option available to you, take it.

Inpatient Treatment

This is a difficult decision for parents to make. This treatment choice has advantages that combine the best of several options available to us, while lacking others. I feel most comfortable recommending intensive inpatient options when the level of abuse or addiction is long-lived, other treatment options have been tried and have failed, or the drug involved is in my 3-D category. For OxyContin, heroin, crack cocaine, crystal meth, opioid pill, or Xanax addictions, I believe it is the only rational response. I also think that eating disorders, suicidal ideation, cutting, harming of self or others, and rage displays all are best served by long-term inpatient attention.

Unlike wilderness camps and outpatient treatment, here we have a chance to isolate our lost one in an environment chosen by us because of its ability to focus exclusively on the addiction at hand. The staff will be trained in the drug's or behavior's long-term effects, and they'll be knowledgeable about what long-term recovery involves.

There is an intensity and singleness of mission present in inpatient treatment that is crucial to success. I think that merely enrolling in the first twenty-eight-day program you find or can afford is a terrible mistake. I need you to give serious thought to your goals and the reality of your lost one's situation. Be thoughtful, effective, and confident in your reasoning and decisions. You are planning for a long-term life of recovery—for everyone.

See chapter 3 for details about how to choose an inpatient treatment program. Look for a program that deals with your lost one's substance abuse or behavior problems and has experience and knowledge regarding it. This should be doable. Next, think about cost and travel distance and visits. Are they important to you, or is quality and depth of experience number one for you? Then you'll need to think about the size of the place, whether or not it's coed, if they have detox onsite if needed, whether a psychiatric component is required because of the nature of the problem, if you need a nurse or doctor involved because of medical or special needs, if you feel comfortable with the facility—its willingness to provide information and its attitude, and, finally, its reputation and experience level. All of this matters to varying degrees. You must decide what is important to you and your lost one.

Also, gender-specific programs are important for young people. As hormonal battlegrounds boys and girls are distracted enough in normal social settings. In crisis, thrust into a new surrounding while emotionally vulnerable or defiant, the last thing they need is a new soul mate or sex partner. The meeting of two troubled minds in intense covenant usually spells more disaster. I am compelled by experience to strongly discourage any such facility, unless it is the only or last resort.

Treatment should never be used as a punishment, nor is it a substitute for parenting. We are not sending an adolescent away, expecting them to grow up or straighten out. Counselors are not all knowing, or better at life than you are. They are better prepared, have critical skills and day-to-day experience that makes them extremely valuable to you and your child.

All of these options will require you and your family to do a great deal of growing, forgiving and learning. It sure beats the alternative.

Jeremy's Story
(Continued from page 117)

Being teachable, and reminding myself that I never know what can happen when the power of an intervention is set loose in the lives of families, is a blessing of the work that I do.

This is the continuing saga of chapter 5's "Jeremy's Story." As I said in the last chapter, this story was far from over. The father suspected Jeremy was smoking crystal meth. As you will remember, Jeremy refused help.

We all agreed that we would stay in touch and be prepared to

(Continued)

swing into action at the first opportunity. Jeremy knew that all he had to do was call and say "I want help," and we were ready.

Nothing happened for quite a while. Each of the family members began attending Al-Anon and gained a great deal of insight. About a year later, Ed, Jeremy's father, called and said that Jeremy's intervention might not have been in vain after all. Ed was nine months sober, attending A.A. meetings, and loving his life!

He had decided that the intervention was probably his! It got even better several months later. Ed called and told Sean and me that Jeremy was under arrest, in jail in California, and that he had had an epiphany: he wanted help! Within a matter of days, Jeremy was out on bail on condition of his full cooperation with our plan, was driven to treatment, and was doing well at the rehab we had chosen.

Father and son are sober, the family has found an amazing opportunity, and Jeremy has a chance to be free in every way, made possible *by sticking to everything* we had decided on, prepared for, and provoked—over a period of years! Never give up hope—we have no idea what is possible.

And by the way, as Sean was preparing to drive off from the county jail to take Jeremy to treatment, Jeremy's mother stopped them and popped her car's trunk. She gestured for me to come over to the car and pointed into the trunk. "Don't forget the bag I packed." In over a year, through the selling of one house and the move to another, two yard sales, and a garage cleaning, she had steadfastly refused to give away, unpack, or touch that duffel bag. She hugged me and quietly said, "As long as that bag was packed, I never lost hope we'd need it one day." Stay ready for a miracle.

THE INTERVENTION

When planning our intervention for a young person, we need to consider when, or if, it is appropriate to involve a girlfriend or boyfriend or a peer. This is problematic. I have seen a friend or romantic partner be helpful, even decisive, in interventions that succeeded. I have also had them become a distraction and interfere with progress—or worse. Asking them to participate presumes that they have a lot of understanding, maturity, and a willingness to break the great teen taboo—snitching. It also risks anger and accusation among the group members.

Also, we need to decide whether the peer was involved in any way with the drug, drink, or behavior that this intervention is all about. Secrets may be involved, and betrayal by a friend can be so disruptive and maddening to the lost one that it derails the process. They have shared guilt but have not been affected in the same way. A close friend or cousin, one who shares a long history with the lost one and has nothing to do with the problem could be a real plus. Obviously, before the intervention, the parent or guardian of any prospective adolescent participant would need to understand and support the mission. I suggest you think long and hard about this question and trust your judgment after talking with the young persons themselves about their feelings and situation.

Siblings often keep the deepest secrets. The participation in interventions by brothers or sisters is always challenging. How close they have been or how involved in the problem the brother or sister has been, needs to be factored in when making these decisions. Older siblings may also be more emotionally able to and intellectually capable of understanding what is going on in the room. For the family, a discussion of all they are bound to learn in the future, and an agreement to put all the destructive secrets on the table with everyone under a forgiveness clause, is important. No one will be reproached or blamed if they come clean now. It will often be the case that an older sibling has been involved in the problem and the secret keeping that has postponed discovery. We do not want to start a round of new anger and shame in our family dynamic. Family secrets are about to be exposed. It is vital to maintain focus and forgiveness.

These meetings can be extremely emotional, wrenching encounters, perhaps not suited to all ages. This is particularly true when the behavior or substance abuse is hardcore or perverse. Use discretion and caution when deciding what would be best for the lost child and for the entire family. When a loved one has made a promise to the lost one, even one as irresponsible as "I'll never tell, no matter what," a lot of damage can be done when the truth comes out.

Whatever other issues emerge as a result of your efforts will be dealt with while the lost one is in treatment. The whole family is finally entering a recovery phase, together. Celebrate the good news, and don't be afraid of what lies ahead. There is already much to be congratulated for: you and your family and friends are about to share the power of truth, love, and courage. Your lost one may well summon courage and face truth for the first time soon also. Don't forget that everyone involved needs to begin their own recovery in some way. What an occasion. What a miracle.

RECOVERY

Next, for kids and families in crisis, is understanding three phases of the recovery plan. You will identify your best treatment option, then give time to deciding whether your teen will come straight home or first have a transitional phase. Sober living houses and the supervised extended care they offer or outpatient treatment might be best for those with severe or long-term problems, before the pressure of home and school.

Finally, we will make a contract for agreement on terms for living back under one roof. The old way clearly failed. Now we will try my way. Trust and responsibility need to be established and earned. You are free to spell out what the expectations are and what the swift and sure consequences of failure are. It is best to trust but always confirm! There will be no negotiation, ever again, regarding relapse, dishonesty, theft, violence, or disappearance. The beauty of these plans is how they are triggered only by facts. The process suspends drama and mystery and replaces them with milestones and the opportunity for achievement and esteem.

For the family of the young person, the future must mean a new vigilance and a higher level of involvement in all aspects of their lives. A lot of thought and discussion needs to take place among the family, and all progress must be celebrated. The entire family needs improved communication, healthy boundaries, and relief. This will be a long, rewarding, and challenging proposition. You must seek support groups and investigate Al-Anon. Do not grow discouraged over setbacks, slips, or normal childish defiance or experiments. Boundaries will be challenged and resolve tested.

It is the nature of adolescence. Never give up hope, and when you win the war, turn to helping others who are in your former hell with their kids.

◦◖◗◦

So, the answer looks like this for your adolescent lost one: having educated yourself on the substance or the behavior involved, you have decided to move forward with an intervention. If you have decided that the problem is so new that a simple confrontation by you alone, with the facts and a treatment option in hand, is enough to start things right, you should be prepared to do that.

If the problem is more severe, you should begin to assemble your intervention team and research the inpatient, outpatient, wilderness program, psychiatric facility, or residential program that best fits your case. As discussed, you'll have to plan for each phase of the adolescent's recovery. Family participation in a meeting, with the consequences statements from your intervention and a contract for transitional living agreements, is a must. Following initial inpatient treatment, there may be a sober living or supervised transitional component, then a return to your home. The eventual return to family life will also need a plan, with lots of talking and listening along the way.

Milestones of achievement are important, and everyone should celebrate progress. Make a big deal of success, and take every chance to have fun as a family. From a trip to the all-star game of their choice to a go-cart race, it doesn't matter how you mark the day, only that you are all involved in the action and that sometimes the found one gets to choose!

7.

THE GOLDEN FEARS

Seniors in Crisis

⚜

The issues that come into play when dealing with seniors in crisis are different from those that involve adults or adolescents.

The aging of the baby boom generation means that our society is about to have its largest percentage of seniors. Aches and pains become a problem as we age and begin to stiffen. We enter the more punishing phase of paying for old injuries or bad habits, such as smoking or being overweight; we suffer through heart surgeries, cancer treatment, a wide range of broken bones, and chronic pain. All of these conditions result in lots of pain medication.

Significant losses are part of aging as well. Losing and burying a lifelong mate is as hard as it gets. But in combination with retirement, a loss of vitality, and separation from family, it can add up to depression, isolation, drinking, drugging, or simply losing the will to go on. While everyone understands that loss and death are very much a part of growing old, that does not mean anyone is prepared for the reality of it happening to them.

The later stages of life bring a gradual erosion of independence, a betrayal by the body, and the certainty that visits to the doctor are going to bring unpleasant or possibly scary news. Most of us won't be granted the boon of simply toddling off to bed, sipping our cocoa, and nodding off to foreverland. I wish it were the case, but no. The family and friends of the aging have a special responsibility to be as respectful and discreet as possible, while acknowledging the seriousness of the situation

Try not to confuse the need for effective pain relief with addiction. Taking pain medication as prescribed and feeling negative effects is not the same as being addicted to pills and using them other than as prescribed. Alcohol is another matter. Drinking may once have been a steady habit, a constant. Growing older and experiencing physical or emotional trauma may mean that what was once a harmless toddy has become a lethal elixir, in a very short time. Talk to your senior, listen to them closely, and try showing up unannounced more often. If you believe there is a crisis, there probably is.

❧ Virginia's Story ❧

Virginia was a seventy-six-year-old woman, comfortably well off and living in an Arizona retirement community. I heard from Sally, a close friend of hers, who called to say that Virginia's bridge club friends had all become concerned about her. Joe, her husband of fifty-some years, had died recently, and since then Virginia had begun to make excuses for missing her usual groups and fun activities with her friends. She was also not answering her phone at night and seemed different.

In a quiet voice Sally asked me if an intervention could work on someone that old and private, or was there no point? I assured her there was reason to hope.

We contacted Virginia's eldest daughter, who lived in California. She agreed to participate, and she and Sally began to plan to meet with the rest of the family.

Virginia had live-in help, a woman who had been a part of the household for years. Rosie was very protective and loyal. As the family began to plan for the intervention, Rosie was consulted and she decided to help. As it turned out, Rosie held the deepest secrets and the key to the future.

Discretion and respect for privacy and dignity are paramount in interventions for the elderly. We decided to have the intervention at the house of another daughter, who lived in the area, since our presence in Virginia's close-knit community might be remarked on. She was invited to lunch, she accepted, and the stage was set. The family was able to afford premium care, and a well-respected national center was chosen, one that specialized in treatment for the elderly.

When Virginia was greeted by her family and her trusted Rosie, she was able to sit and listen to all they had to say. The critical moments were when Rosie revealed to the family that Virginia was not only drinking every night but also abusing prescription drugs. She turned to Virginia and begged her to get help and not to leave her. Virginia accepted.

(Continued)

145

> Virginia's underlying issues were her grief over the death of her husband, her loneliness, and her fears of growing old alone. Her treatment center was able to help her in all of these areas, as well as her drug and alcohol abuse—actually symptoms of her real issues.
>
> With the help of a close circle of old friends, her family, and her trusted helper, Virginia was able to finish treatment and return to an active, full life. And I hear she is a terror at the bridge table!

TREATMENT OPTIONS FOR SENIORS

There are treatment centers around the country with specific programs for geriatric addiction and behavioral problems. There are not enough to suit me, but I understand how difficult and costly such care is. For this growing segment of our population, treatment of addiction, psychiatric illness, and pain management is wrapped up in other concerns, all of which I want to address with you now.

Often the crisis point comes as a result of grief or depression following the loss of a lifelong partner or job. Isolation and loneliness are huge factors in geriatric alcoholism and addiction. These same life events may start dementia or other psychiatric breaks or accelerate them dramatically. It is a sad time and one that has echoes of your own future and mortality as well. All of this has to be recognized and included in our plan for recovery, if we hope to succeed.

All medical conditions need to be noted and shared with prospective treatment facilities in order to ensure that they are staffed to handle your needs. I urge you to make sure that the facility understands the complete medical picture. Generally, there is trust between an older person and a doctor, and that physician's help could be most important. If not involved beforehand, certainly you want them onboard as soon as possible. I recommend a review of medications after treatment as well, so that any inappropriate narcotics or other meds may be phased out or discontinued.

The best programs for seniors already know all of this and are willing and able to address the gamut of these issues. Talk with them. Take note of the places that have the longest history of geriatric care, those with hospital affiliations, and especially those facilities that include psychological evaluation, detox, transitional components, and live-in additional programs all in one place. Everything takes a little longer and moves a little slower for these folks—including recovery. The facility that is able to deal with more than the addiction or behavior in question and to address the entire spectrum of problems and challenges will be your best choice.

There is the question of insurance. Losing an insurance policy at an advanced age is a horrifying thought. I want you to understand how difficult replacing medical insurance may be at the age of sixty-five or beyond. You need to be hyperaware of the policy, its benefits and its limitations. If you intend to use insurance, do a lot of upfront work with the treatment center, and take your cue from their advice and experience. Self-pay, or Medicare if it's an option, may be best in a situation in which the treatment cost may be cause for termination or review, particularly if there are other preexisting illnesses or matters being treated through the policy. Talk to insurance agents, doctors, and facilities and get up-to-the-minute counsel and direction. Always double-check each piece of information.

So, for seniors, you'll need to find the right detox and treatment facility, while balancing the need for rehab against the complicating factors of age, health, medications, psychological state, pain, and emotional trauma.

I urge you to visit your choices and to speak at length with the staff and alumni whenever possible. Obviously, the facility that has experience with seniors may be the best. Unlike other treatment processes, that of your senior lost one may require frequent visits and communication, as well as little reassurances by mail or phone during their stay.

Outpatient Treatment

Outpatient treatment may be a viable first response if there is a convenient option close to home. If your lost one's doctor has an affiliation at a hospital that offers outpatient services, for example, this could be very positive. For an elderly person who is still relatively independent, living alone, or just not faced with the other complications of aging, outpatient treatment will be an easier "sell" and less threatening. And a good way of getting them out of the house and back into showing up.

Inpatient Treatment

For most of you, the thought of intervening occurred because you became worried enough to try something drastic. This means that inpatient treatment is probably going to be best, in the face of serious drinking, pill dependence, diminished mental and physical capacity, gambling, or depression. For inpatient treatment for seniors combined with detox, I feel comfortable recommending the minimum stay.

INTERVENTIONS FOR SENIORS

This intervention can be a far more sedate and small affair. There may not be a need for the kind of production involved in other interventions, such as letters of consequence.

Interventions are hard to face when our kids or our mate are involved. The emotional toll can be even greater with seniors in crisis. The reasons are easy to understand but difficult to deal with. First, the most important life issues for our aging loved ones are security and independence. Both are under siege in the intervention process. These biggest fears of our aged have to be taken into respectful account throughout the intervention plan and staging. You may well be their only advocate. Think about that and the responsibility it implies. Their introduction to recovery is in your hands, and the way they are approached may well spell the difference between success and failure.

In the face of loss of mental function, physical deterioration, or emotional breakdown, faster is better. The faster you can address and deal with the diagnosis and what it means for the future, the better off everyone will be. This is the most heartbreaking intervention of all, when the lost one may remain lost forever. Even though your lost one may never understand what has happened, you and your family will be well served by observing the ritual, making the plans, advising them of your concerns and intentions, and bearing the confusion, accusation, or tears of rage or pain as best you can. You have to know in your heart that you are doing the right thing, for everyone concerned. I cannot imagine a more difficult conversation between generations, which makes your determination to do the right thing all the more honorable. At that point your actions are designed to reassure yourself and your family and to demonstrate for the record how things were done.

Involving the spouse of an aged addict or alcoholic may be problematic if there are mental illness, heart problems, medical considerations, or other extenuating concerns. An additional concern is forcing a spouse to keep secrets. It is best, I feel, to allow the spouse to participate only if they are determined to do so, and then only if you agree it is appropriate. They must, of course, be allowed ample time for good-byes and solace in each other's affection.

While the lost one is at treatment is the best time—with everyone involved—to deal with the unresolved questions of how fit the lost one is to return to their present living situation and how they will be helped in the future. Allowing a senior the time and dignity to recover and begin anew is a privilege and among your finest efforts on earth, but it is also a nerve-wracking and tiring challenge. They can be unpredictable and cranky—on a good day!

Loss of independence is a big issue for seniors facing an intervention. No one wants to go away, do the work of getting sober, and return only to be told that they will not have the same privilege or freedom they enjoyed before doing all that work. It is unfair, even punitive, to find these results on returning home. This will, however, be a necessary discussion in a large number of interventions on seniors.

When addiction or mental illness strikes an older person, the medical, psychological, and emotional repercussions can be lifelong. A parent or grandparent who isn't living under your roof may be unable to continue life alone. This may be brought to the fore by the intervention and the discovery it fosters. You may have known something needed doing before the crisis and simply not had sufficient warning of how dire things had become. My experience tells me that when most families intervene in the case if a senior, the next discussion is about how they will live after treatment. These are simple facts. I want to stress the three things you need to hold in mind here: respect, dignity, and love. Are these always important in interventions? Yes. Are they most important when dealing with old people? You better believe it.

Also, you may have grown used to the idea of a parent being able to fend for themselves or even help you out. They may be babysitting, house-watching, driving machines who are always available. They may have helped you to buy your home or they may have lent you money over the years. Psychologically, we think of our parents or grandparents as frozen in time. They raised us, they made a life for themselves, and they helped us do the same. Now things are changing, and often they are changing faster than we realize.

❁

Even with the special circumstances involved staging in intervention for a senior, it is important to keep in mind that the goal is identical to that of other interventions: an admission of the problem and an agreement to accept treatment now. Just remember: respect, dignity, and love.

8.

IT'S YOUR TURN

Your *Recovery*

❧

So it has happened! I hope that the intervention did everyone in the room some good. I know that whatever happened, you and your family and friends will never be the same, not on this subject. You have learned some important facts and grown together. I hope the lost one got found by you. I hope they are away at treatment as you are reading this. But regardless of my hopes and whatever happened, here's what needs to happen next: homework.

That's right: regardless of the intervention's seeming success or failure, you must continue along *your path* to recovery and acceptance. Know that your future is in your hands. You need to be prepared and thoughtful about your next moves. When an intervention does not end in a trip to rehab or treatment, the tables have been turned: Are you all serious? Will you hang together and see this through? The addict wants to know. They desperately need to defeat the threat they perceive.

In truth, there is often more than one intervention, masquerading as episodes in the wake of the actual event. The ongoing application of your consequences statement is another intervention. The refusal of the enablers to break is the next. Then life will begin to whittle down the lost one and confront them, finally, with the real cost without rescue by their former hostages. An awesome intervention happens again. The law may arrive, hosting a really effective intervention—with no regret or fear. All of this and more is on your side of the equation. Don't give up. Give it over to a higher power, fate, destiny—whatever you can hold on to. This works.

I want you to know what I see families do most often after their lost one enters treatment: nothing. The family will get a well-deserved good night's sleep. The mom will cry, letting out months or years of frustration and worry. Everybody hugs, and there is some much-needed laughter. I see relief and exhilaration. Occasionally, I'll get a call of thanks. Once in a while I'll get a follow-up call months later, usually if things are really good or really bad. That's about it. Why? What is going on here?

Often, addicts and alcoholics are able to bear the trials and disgrace of their behavior. They tell themselves that everything will be fine, while the fears and panic are put down by a reassuring hit, drink, or behavior. They tell themselves to focus on this one accomplishment, one event that guarantees relief and a magical start to success. This is why it is so important to move to treatment immediately from the intervention. What they have told themselves has superseded the genuine emotional clarity they held for a brief moment, while they were surrounded by concern and love. But given a moment's chance, all of that will wilt in the face of the demand, so deep inside them, for relief and power.

Given the opportunity, in this vulnerable state, they will refute their commitment and escape the grasp of the group, dismissing the group's concerns as hysteria, and they'll laugh outwardly at their moment of clarity. This is what my experience tells me. Give an addict or alcoholic in trouble a couple of nights' sleep, a couple of bucks, a meal, and maybe some sex (if *they* feel like it), and everything is cool again. I'm a new man, and the new man needs a drink!

Families have their own version of this delusional system. Somewhere along the line you may have thought of treatment as "the answer," and so it became a goal. As you became informed and began to learn what was possible, you found hope. Eventually, you shared this with other people and took heart. Feeling more positive and prepared, you actually made a decision.

At some point, probably in the midst of all your work, you began to believe. After the intervention, the relief was amazing. I think it is one of the great moments in our lives, actually making a difference in our home and family. The elation is intoxicating.

But here's what I know: treatment centers don't create recovery. They create a period of sobriety or abstinence—from substances or behaviors—that provides time and security for everybody concerned, nothing more. They provide a new environment that furnishes healthy routines, backed by consistent feedback and discipline. That's a big deal, and it's important for a good start on your new life. But much more is called for if you want a healthy change in your life and home. I am not raining on your parade here—I'm just offering you an umbrella and a weather report: there are storms ahead.

WHILE THEY'RE AWAY:
THE LOST ONE AT TREATMENT

When your lost one left for treatment, they were undoubtedly having mixed feelings. I believe some part of any lost one is relieved to get help. They are feeling a lot of other things as well. It is an intense time for everybody but an incredibly hard thing for the lost one. Courage, desperation, fear are on display here. No one involved knows what to expect. Here is what I think you need to think about and plan for.

Old behavior is the product of intensely held beliefs: beliefs about how the world works and, more important, about how we get what we want and need. There is no evidence in my work that suggests having a meeting and packing a suitcase changes any of a family's oldest ideas and behaviors. Nor does reading a book, even one as brilliant and perceptive as this one. You, your family, and the lost one will need to change old ideas and behaviors if you hope to sustain the progress you have made. This time away at treatment or this time of outpatient therapy must be combined with new behaviors, new ways of communicating, and better thinking. One of the twelve-step program axioms that I like is "I can't think my way to better living, but I can live my way to better thinking." If you work at it and give one another time to change while living by a new plan, your thinking can change. I guarantee your feelings will change as well.

Treatment will introduce your lost one to some truth about their condition, insight into how to treat it, and, I hope, advice and direction on plans for the future. There will be a routine and requirements in place, rules and expectations that must be met if the lost one intends to stay. Most of the time, the lost one does not like this change. Addicts, alcoholics, and mentally ill people whose regimens have been interrupted and exposed are generally not happy about the interference. At some point their old behavior will reappear. Your lost one was lost in a world of lies and self-destruction, a very selfish world where their needs and demands were more important than anything else in the world, including rules, expectations, love, responsibilities, children, jobs, parents, and others. It all looked the same to them after awhile. Reality became an oppressive, unhappy place from which to flee at the first opportunity.

This immature, selfish behavior is bound to come back, demanding sympathy and a way out. After all, attention getting through negative behavior was learned and rewarded in the old family dynamic. You or others in the family or group may get a phone call from the treatment facility complaining of a variety of outrages or bad feelings, all designed to justify leaving and coming home. You will need to follow the plan and stick to the consequences.

Since the recovery business is so big and growing so fast, there are places that are not very good, poorly staffed, or run by incompetents or charlatans. As in any other industry, there is good and bad. Unfortunately, in this business we are dealing with the lives of people in crisis, people who may get only one chance to find help.

So, if you get the "I can't stay here" call, you need to listen to the lost one's complaints. Note them and ask if you can call back in awhile. Buy time and don't be sarcastic, threatening, or angry. Briefly remind the lost one of the consequences of refusing treatment and assure them you are taking this seriously. Then call the treatment center and ask for the lost one's primary counselor. If they are not available, ask for a head honcho. Tell them about your concerns, making it plain that the lost one is talking about leaving. Listen to the responses to your lost one's complaints and decide how you feel. If the place suddenly sounds wacky or unreasonable, it is possible your lost one is in the wrong place. On the other hand, if you understand and accept what you are hearing and realize that the lost one is seeking a way out, ask the counselor to arrange a phone meeting with you, the lost one, and them. If the lost one refuses such a meeting, tell the counselor to read the consequences of refusal to the lost one in their entirety and make it clear that they have not changed. Remember: this is precisely why those statements were handed over to the facility in the first place. Everyone has the same information, and the lost one knows it! You are done.

The rest of your group has to understand and agree to this as well. The lost one will not give up until they are convinced that they are beaten. If they insist on leaving treatment, do not send money or buy an airline or bus ticket. Do not allow them to return home. If you need a restraining order, get one. You are entering the crucial phase of your lost one's journey now, and you must be strong and sure. Everyone has to hold firm, or all is lost. If they stay, you have posted a major victory, meaning what you said and valuing your family and your own life.

I suggest that you not call the facility at all during the first month. Let the center and its staff, along with your lost one, do their job. You have plenty to do at home, so does the lost one at treatment. Send cards and letters of encouragement and reassurance. Be supportive and interested. Encourage others to do the same. Plan visits when allowed and convenient, especially with the kids, if they wish to go. Family week or whatever family program exists at your choice of facilities is vital! Do not write the lost one about what they are missing, and don't rehash old scenes. Be upbeat and brief, sharing any happiness or dreams that you feel safe talking about. Encourage, encourage, encourage.

Hopefully, addicts and alcoholics in treatment are being exposed to twelve-step literature and practices. They may attend meetings of twelve-step groups and work the steps while at treatment. But as hard as this is for me to say, twelve-step recovery programs may not be for everyone. This is not the only way to go, but I must tell you, after decades of sobriety and work in the field, I don't know an easier, softer, more effective program of recovery than the one outlined in the A.A. book and their literature. I don't know a more successful approach.

If the facility that you chose is faith-based, that's fine. Whatever they are, I hope they have a family program as part of their process. If they do, participate. Use the statements from the intervention as a basis for discussion. This discussion needs to be aimed at forging agreements that apply to the day you are reunited. This is essential. Return to the lives of loved ones and friends has to be conditional and thoughtfully designed.

However lengthy or short the treatment program is, it is the time for everyone to address their problems. Give the process time and let it work. When the lost one calls irritated or sad, empathize and listen to them. Share some of your frustration or tell them how you miss them too, but gently remind them what is at stake, how proud you are, and how you are sure their day will be better tomorrow. Limit your phone time, and always ask the facility when the phone hours are so that you know when and how often these calls are appropriate.

YOUR RECOVERY

Now, what exactly are you doing to recover? Your old ideas and behavior may need some attention as well. You and your family have been through the wringer. Mistakes were made and sometimes ugly things were said and done, sometimes by you. Now is the time to address some of your own issues, such as the inability to trust your lost one, resentment, anger, doubt, and a host of other common worries.

I have no useful insight into why people do not attend Al-Anon meetings when they can be so helpful, but many don't. I strongly recommend that you find one and attend it or its equivalent soon and often. There are specific support groups for families of addicts as well, known as Nar-Anon. Whatever your lost one is in treatment for, there is a support group out there for their families. Get there. Listen, identify, get the literature, read up, stick your hand out, and participate.

There are only a couple of reasons not to go: you don't intend to recover, or you think it's not your problem, or that you have done enough. I wish you good luck with that.

There are programs for teens, kids, and adults. These are Al-Ateen, Al-Atot, and Al-Anon. I'd say they basically have it covered: from child-care meetings to teen support, your whole family has an opportunity to learn and cope and, more important, recover. Whether you take advantage of this or not is your decision, but it will affect everyone's chances. I also urge you, if you choose not to attend support groups, to seek whatever counseling you can afford. Find a therapist or counselor you trust and talk to them about your experiences and your feelings. Be open and honest.

Give yourself some help and attention and do the same for your kids or other involved family members.

While your lost one is away and you are helping yourself, find some brief time alone or with friends each day to simply stop. Think about something besides the drama. I think it's important to recognize how long it's been since you had some fun. Especially if you have kids, a break is called for. Find some time for ice cream and the park, or anything you know they love to do. Same for you.

Stay in touch with the others who participated in the intervention. Update them on things and share what's going on with you. You can even issue weekly updates via e-mail, if you wish.

Finally, plan something for the lost one's return. Nothing elaborate, just some idea or observation that they agree with would be nice. A meal together, maybe doing the ride back from treatment together, or some time alone. However strange or brief this time may be, make something out of it, if it's doable.

9.

LOST AND FOUND

Post-Treatment Recovery

❧

It is, I believe, peculiar to human consciousness to be able to hold opposing feelings in the same mind. So it is with the return of a loved one from recovery.

What we're talking about is this simple: more change. Families and groups learn comfort in the known and often recoil from the unknown—no matter how dreadful the known seems to an outsider. Wives or girlfriends may not have known a sober husband in quite awhile. A husband may not remember when his wife was last accountable and clear-eyed. Parents will be simultaneously full of anxiety and excitement, not knowing what to expect. Many times everyone involved is "off the map," outside their comfort zone.

I understand. Even though a return home is a wonderful milestone, it is fraught with memory of bad times. Sometimes resentment simmers in the rest of the family: the lost one stayed loaded, screwed everyone over, stole, and lied—and got a paid vacation, while we struggled on alone! There is a lot at play here, so let's take a look at some of what we can expect and how we can best move forward together.

I told you there were storms coming. If, so far, all has been sweetness and light, that's marvelous. I am so pleased for you. There are times when everything seems to come together and good people get a break. If some of what we have covered has already happened, then you can appreciate how important preparation is. Either way, we are here now. It is a new phase of life for everybody involved, and I want you all to get maximum benefit from this opportunity. Let's go over what we can do to help everybody get what they need.

The return of the found one is a big deal. Everyone is likely to have expectations and fears aplenty. In most cases, there is very little open discussion regarding these feelings. That is not going to happen in your home though. I want you to have an agreement in place—one forged during treatment—that lays out what you expect life to look like after treatment. It addresses the exit plan that the found one worked on before they left treatment. If they don't have one, we'll make one up. For addicts and alcoholics, the normal recommendation is attending ninety meetings in ninety days. That does not mean going to four on Saturday and three on Sunday. That means a meeting or two a day, consistently, for the first ninety days out of treatment. It is not your job to find these meetings, drive the found one, or pick them up. You may do all of these if it is necessary, but the primary responsibility needs to be transferred back where it belongs.

If a twelve-step program is to be effective, the basic tenets should be in place. A sponsor is someone who is available to guide the newcomer through the literature and principles of A.A., who will work the steps with the found one and offer guidance in a general way. A sponsor is vital. Simply saying that you are in A.A. does not mean anything is happening. Being *in* something means following the program, actively progressing through the book and the steps, and making efforts toward a new life. These include paying bills and debts, being accountable, making amends to people, and helping others. This is all common-sense stuff that yields real benefits.

Trust needs to be earned and built slowly by demonstration, not conversation. Do not listen to what the found one says: watch what they do. This is who they are. Make plain your conditions for acceptance in the home: no repeat of the addiction or behavior that began all of this, no more lies, no more fits of anger or sulking, no verbal or physical attacks, no disappearing. Only drug tests and a Breathalyzer can confirm sobriety. Use them frequently and randomly. This can lead to a lot of disagreement, but, seriously, who is the only person afraid of a drug or alcohol test? Right. I understand that this may seem distrusting or demeaning. Why is there distrust in the first place? How long were you and yours demeaned and dismissed by the lost one and their actions? Either these things matter to you both or they do not. Why be afraid to find out? Being afraid or confused, compromising your beliefs and your self-respect, living a lie—that was the old system. If you want it back, be sure to ignore all of what I'm saying here. Any and all of these concerns, or any that are not here, should be included in your agreement. This is your declaration of what is expected and what will not be tolerated. Tailor it thoughtfully. This will work for everyone's benefit, especially the found one's.

The found one is going to be under the microscope for a while.

They do not need to like it; they need to understand and accept it. They earned all of this and more. Families torn apart by deceit and dark secrets, drug abuse, alcoholism, or mental illness have lots of wounds, some still fresh. Time and sustained good behavior are the only real healers. Ronald Reagan got it right when he suggested suspicious parties can be trusted, but with confirmation. I *do not* want you to become a snoop, a nag, or a detective. I *do* want you to be vigilant and behave as if your life and the lives of your family matter to you.

While the found one was lost, a lot of responsibility and authority may have been taken from them. They were unreliable, unpredictable, or worse. It is only natural that tensions will arise now that they are back. They may feel entitled to an immediate return to normalcy without question or accomplishment. You may be resistant to these roles. All of this needs discussion and understanding. Make time to review the week and unwind together. Make it important, and start always by examining your own faults and shortcomings. Try to identify any positives, and try to find some humor in the situation, if possible. Work together.

All recovery has milestones and phases. I encourage you to celebrate each milestone, each accomplishment. There are "double winner" meetings that you and the found one can attend together. Twelve-step programs give out chips marking thirty, sixty, and ninety days sober, as well as six- and nine-month chips, coins, or medallions. Sober birthdays are celebrated with cakes and candles at some meetings. Go to these "open meetings" and remember how things were awhile back. Feel good and express joy and gratitude. You all earned it. Furthermore, find reasons to be together as a family and find some fun as often as possible. Laughter and closeness will go a long way toward happiness and recovery. What did we go through all of this for?

Remember life before the drama. Remember the dreams and hopes, the good times, and what could have been. This is a *new beginning*, so try a *new way*. Mutual respect, patient conversation, and lots of time and space: these are the orders of the day. Money, work, sex, child rearing, and communication—these are the most common causes of disagreement and hurt feelings. If you or your family are disappointed in the found one's lack of attention or attitude, give it time. If the found one is suddenly obsessed with work or a TV program, let it be for now. Things have certainly been worse. All things run in cycles. Each of you will have good days with bad moments and bad days with good moments. Each will argue or flare up, and inevitably each will revisit the previous sins of the other. This is unfortunate, but it does not have to spell failure. Give this new way a real chance, and pay attention to your own backyard.

Sit down together and read the chapter called "The Family Afterward" in the Big Book of A.A. It is a master work, exhaustive and brilliant in its even-handed characterization of all that is going on in a recovering home. I dare you to read it together. It will take twenty minutes and evoke lots of laughter and conversation. Its entire slant is that a lot has occurred in a short time, much of it intense. That means that a lot is up for grabs within the family dynamic—going from distrust to misunderstanding to raging fire is not a long trip in this atmosphere. There has been much confusion; everyone is tense and a little sensitive. Hell, a lot sensitive is more like it. All of these feelings and needs will be better dealt with if talked about openly and with some sense of proportion.

Take it easy on one another and see what is possible when a goal is truly shared. Try to compromise wherever possible, and be quick to show your support of and pleasure in your newly found one. Intimacy may be slow to return to what it once was in a marriage or relationship. Newly found adolescents are especially eager to get back freedom and privacy. They must earn it.

Pick your battles. If the found one is doing what needs to be done, chastising them for other shortcomings is a bad strategy. For the first year or so of recovery, the actual process of recovery should by rights be *priority one*. Not better grades, not a haircut, not getting back on the football team. Decide what is actually important and try to lighten up some.

Particularly for young people, old associates and hangouts are bad news. I understand what is meant by "if you hang around the barbershop, sooner or later you're gonna get a haircut." Disassociating from "using buddies," separating from negative or toxic friendships, avoiding old haunts, or dropping out of the cool scene are the hardest things for an alcoholic or addict to do, much less a kid. It is important that the found one understand how vital these agreements are. Get to them through give and take, be loving and firm. Tell the found one openly what your fears are, what the rules for living here will be, how you feel about having them back, and then go about your business. Hope for the best, but prepare for the worst.

RELAPSE

This thought brings us logically to our final discussion of the chapter. The topic of relapse is fraught with controversy and ignorance.

When relapse is considered and discussed, emotions run deep and opinions are plentiful. For our purposes we need to understand only a couple of ideas.

"Relapse is a part of recovery." I hear that a lot around the recovery community, and I could not disagree more. Relapse is a symptom of disease and of human nature. It is not peculiar to addicts and alcoholics. It is, in fact, common among diabetics, heart patients, tuberculars, and all manner of people suffering restrictions due to illness. It simply means returning to a self-destructive or negative behavior after a period of abstinence. For you, it means the reliving of a nightmare and the dashing of your hopes. Do not let this be the case.

Many people have struggled, relapsed, begun anew, and eventually triumphed. You need to be prepared and have an understanding with the found one about the responses that are built into a relapse. Having a plan means talking about it, first at the treatment center and then at home. Having such an agreement also means not having to go through all the drama, recriminations, and fighting that are often provoked by relapse. Simply do what has been agreed upon, swiftly and surely. If the circumstances are peculiar or you feel some mitigating factor is involved, feel free to adjust your response.

I want to note that the organization that I have sited as so effective in combating addiction and alcoholism—A.A.—has *only one requirement* for membership: *a desire* to stop drinking. Not success, not a promise, nothing. If that is all they need to love and accept members back, time and again, then surely we can learn to love those who fail, even fail repeatedly, without bearing the brunt of the emotional, legal, financial, and medical costs they accrue.

Also, not every relapse is the same. Think about it: if I am sober for, say, ten months, and all signs are positive, and progress is evident in all phases of my life, but then my dog dies, I break my leg, the paperboy skips me on Sunday, and I sneak a beer—is that really the same as getting out of treatment and scoring some heroin a week later, overdosing, and wrecking my mom's car? I don't think so. Let's all try to grasp some of what is involved here: perspective, progress, compassion, and practical boundaries all foster mental health and open communication. Everyone who is willing to try, who corrects behavior after each mistake, and who sincerely acknowledges error and supports common goals deserves another chance. Not constant money for bail or drug bills, not free rent, not a car—a chance. As a result of our work together through this journey, I believe we all agree on what real love and compassion look like now.

In all relapses, the last thing that occurs is the actual use or behavior. So much has to occur prior to that act: all the good in the found one's life has to be rejected out of hand, love for all around them has to be discounted, shame has to be accepted, immaturity indulged, and fear allowed to rule their actions. It is a nightmare journey. Furthermore, they must cast aside all the work they have done, their friends in A.A., their accomplishments and pride. Do you see now how powerful and mysterious these obsessions are? They are a pestilence without end for humans everywhere.

If my twenty-year-old son is recovering from a long-term heroin addiction and I find out he had a drink on a Saturday night after a year of recovery, I am probably not going to rush back to treatment or throw him out of the house. I am going to talk with him and the rest of the family, decide what the proper response is for us as a family, and present him with the consequences. I would do so in a family meeting that acknowledges the seriousness of the offense, but also with context and perspective. Then my son would accept or reject the consequences. Rejection means he has to go. I cannot support a refusal of responsibility; nor will I allow him to disrespect our past suffering and sacrifice. My family and my happiness are as important as his rights. If he accepts, then I owe him my best effort at getting past the failure. I have to empathize.

Relapse is a distinct possibility, no matter how well we have all done or how hard we have tried. Remember: this thing that took your found one had enough power to take over their lives, deny your claim on them, and put them beyond the reach of normal love and concern. It is logical that it has not lost all power in a matter of days, weeks, or months. The habits and beliefs born of a lifetime or a dark journey are not easily erased. There is much wisdom in the phrase "One day at a time."

❧

I want to close on a positive note. In all my years of work in this field, I have come not to hope for miracles but to expect them. Sean agrees with me. We know that any life can be reclaimed, any lost one found, no matter how hopeless things appear—because of the combined power of knowledge, love, and action. When out-of-whack systems finally begin to recognize and repair their most damaged parts, things slowly begin to right themselves. Progress breeds hope, hope breeds faith, faith begets confidence, and results add up. Basically, all decent humans long to be accepted, valued, and useful. It is inherent in all healthy people. When poison is introduced, lives are lost. We have the power, each of us, to organize and follow a process that will unleash a world of possibilities and opportunities for healing and recovery *that would not otherwise be possible!*

I want to remind you one last time that what we preach we have practiced thousands of times. I know that what lies at the core of the miracle of true, sustained recovery is confronting the facts of our tragedy and finding unity through the truth. By forcing the lost one and their loved ones to face the inevitable consequences of self-destruction before death can occur, something deeply spiritual and mysterious begins: transformation and redemption through grace. The beauty of what I and countless others do in all the fields touched by this epidemic is that some of you, who will be granted a miracle through your intervention, will give back in unbelievable ways the knowledge and dedication that was given to you by others. We have a fighting chance. There are so many wonderful people out there ready to help and guide you, so many resources available, and now you have really started to find and work with them. Never stop asking questions and looking for the help you need. You never need to do anything alone again. Congratulations on your courage. I am proud of you. I guarantee you are on your way to something profoundly different from where you were the day you opened our book. It has been such an honor and a privilege to spend this time with you. Thank you for trusting me at such a difficult and painful time.

APPENDIX

A Home Contract for Adolescents

Recovery Responsibilities

You are required to attend _____ twelve-step meetings a week.

Please list the meetings you plan to attend:

_____

_____

_____

You must obtain a sponsor in a twelve-step program by _____.

Consequence: _____

_____

_____

Complete abstinence from all mind-altering substances is a requirement. If you use drugs or alcohol, the following consequences will take place:

Consequence: _____
_____
_____

MEDICATIONS
It is your responsibility to take any and all medications that have been prescribed to you by your doctor. It is also your responsibility to tell someone if you are experiencing any strange side effects.

Consequence: _____
_____
_____

COMMUNICATIONS
It is important to remain open and respectful in your communication with your family. Your family is not made up of mind readers. Talk about what is going on inside you. It is okay to get angry. It is not okay to cuss, scream, throw things, have a temper tantrum, etc.

Consequence: _____
_____
_____

CURFEW
Weeknights _____ A.M./P.M.
Weekends _____ A.M./P.M.

These curfews hours are your responsibility to follow and only yours! However, they may be negotiated depending on whether you are at your meetings and/or other appropriate outings. This will be decided by your parent(s). You must notify them of your outings *beforehand* in order to get approval!

Consequence: _____

_____

_____

CHORES

1. _____
2. _____
3. _____
4. _____
5. _____
6. _____

Consequence: _____

_____

_____

SCHOOL BEHAVIOR

In becoming responsible for the changes in my life, I will attend all of my classes everyday. This responsibility will include following all school rules and showing appropriate behavior inside and outside the classroom.

I will also maintain satisfactory grades, "C" or better, as part of my school performance.

Consequence: _____

_____

_____

OTHER CONDITIONS

_____

_____

Consequence: _____

_____

_____

PARENTS

As part of the program, you are required to be an active participant in establishing and maintaining a healthy environment in your home. That is why we require that you continue to follow through with what you learn in this program. Do not expect anything from your teen that you are not willing to do yourself! Remember that a healthy environment should start within our own homes!

❧

This contract is renegotiable after ninety days. Your responsible behavior will determine what the next contract will contain. Remember what you have learned in this program and put it to good use. *It works only if you work it!*

As with all contracts, you and your parents must sign this. Your signature will indicate that you are willing to follow this contract before you give it your signature.

Teenager: _____   Date: _____

Parent: _____   Date: _____

Parent: _____   Date: _____

Witness: _____

RESOURCES

National Council On Alcoholism
www.recoverycentral.org
800-729-6686
This organization is nationwide, and each state has its own agency. They have a twenty-four-hour staff and vast knowledge of all the resources available to you.

U.S. Drug Rehab Center
www.usdrugrehabcenters.com
866-449-1490
A locating service with over 14,000 rehab listings.

Recovery Connection
www.recoveryconnection.org
800-993-3869
This organization has qualified staff across the country available twenty-four-hours a day to answer all concerns regarding addiction.

SAMHSA (Substance Abuse and Mental Health Services Administration)
www.samhsa.gov
240-276-2750 or 800-662-HELP
This is a national government-sponsored clearinghouse. Also affiliated with them is the Center for Substance Abuse Treatment, which helps find community-based treatment services for those who need them. They are online at http://www.csat. samhsa.gov.

Also under their umbrella is a directory of treatment programs. This is at wwwfindtreatment.samhsa.gov.

Salvation Army
www.salvationarmyusa.org
Check your phone book for local numbers.
For low-cost or no-cost treatment.

National Veterans Administration
www.nvf.org
877-777-4443

American Council on Alcoholism
www.aca-usa.org
800-527-5344
For information about adolescents in crisis, go to http://ncadi.samhsa.gov/ govpubs/rpo996/

Try this site for seniors in crisis; it is affiliated with CAMH, Center for Addiction and Mental Health: www.camh.net/Publications/Strategic_Plan ning_Annual_Reports/Annual_Reports/2007/ar07_older_people.html

Also try this site, which is a treasure trove of resources, info information, and links. Also government-sponsored through the Council on Aging: www.ncoa.org/Downloads/PromotingOlderAdultHealth.pdf

Resources

American Self-Help Sourcebook
www.mentalhealth.net/selfhelp
973-326-6789
A database and national self-help guide to multiple support groups for addiction, bereavement, health, mental health, disabilities, abuse, parenting, caregiver concerns, and other stressful life situations.

Alcoholics Anonymous
www.aa.org
212-870-3400, or check your phone book for your local listing.

Al-Anon
www.al-anon.alateen.org
888-425-2666, or check your phone book for your local listing.
Support for families and friends of alcoholics.

Narcotics Anonymous
www.na.org
818-773-999, or check your phone book for your local listing.

Nar-Anon
www.nar-anon.org
800-477-6291
Support for families and friends of drug abusers.

Gamblers Anonymous
www.ga.org
(213) 386-8789

National Council of Problem Gambling
www.ncpgambling.org
800-522-4700

Cocaine Anonymous
www.ca.org
800-347-8998

Dual Recovery Anonymous
www.draonline.org
877-883-2332
Help for those with co-occurring illnesses or addictions.

Overeaters Anonymous
www.oa.org/index.htm
505-891-2664
A support and guidance resource for eating disorders

Sex Addicts Anonymous
www.saa.org
800-477-8191

Mental Health of America Online
www.nmha.org
800-969-6642
For psychiatric crisis or mental illness.

National Institute of Mental Health
www.nimhinfo@nih.gov
301-443-4513 (local), or 1-866-615-6464 (toll-free), or 301-443-8431
(TTY), or 1-866-415-8051 (TTY toll-free)
A resource guide for mental health treatment.

The Lesbian, Gay, Bisexual, and Transgender Community Center
www.gaycenter.org
212-620-7310

Cybersober.com
www.cybersober.com
Maps and directions to 133,000 twelve-step meetings.

Anonymousone.com
www.anonymousone.com
A database of international and regional twelve-step meetings, sober clubs, treatment centers, and much more.

Drugs.com
www.drugs.com/pill_identification.html
Good for online pill identification.

ACKNOWLEDGMENTS

Candy wishes to acknowledge:

My husband, Mike (and they said it wouldn't last!), and our children: Bridget and Kelly. You have always made me happy and proud!

Sean Finnigan, better known as chicken-yellow-baby-brat . . . not anymore!!

Ed Storti, for bringing such dignity and class to our profession.

My mentor, Dr. James Fearing, who predicted the future when he said: "With you, Candy, the circus is always in town."

Dr. David Kipper, for his dedication to the disease of addiction . . . and me!

The Ladies of Landale, Toad, Emmy, and the "Big Ten."

And to all the folks in all the rooms, that saved me and countless others.

Sam Mettler, creator of "Intervention," for bringing the power of intervention to A&E television, and to all the support and production staff at GRB Entertainment.

Shelly Schultz, a mensch, who helped us make this dream come true!

Eileen Cope, and everyone at Trident Media. You were our guide and our champion. You helped make this book a reality.

Jeff Galas, our editor at Avery. We trusted you with our baby and you made us proud parents.

We must thank all the families, over the years, for allowing us the privilege of being there when the miracle happened. Thank you all for letting us be of service.

Finally to all the dedicated professionals and volunteers in the field: You inspire and sustain us. Any mistakes or omissions are entirely the responsibility and fault of the authors, not the many men and women who shared their expertise and knowledge so generously with us in the course of our research. Thank you all for your patience, answers, suggestions, and time. From the national Drug Czar to the man or woman making a twelve-step call, you are heroes all.

We are most grateful for the Irish gift that keeps on giving: the Blarney that Blessed us all!

Sean wishes to acknowledge:

Robb Royer, a leader by example and an amazing friend and partner.

Acknowledgments

The Men of Troy

My brothers, Chris and Mike, and their families. With them I had a chance. Their support and encouragement over so many years saved my life. Simply the best brothers a man ever had.

My father, John Finnigan. Because of him, I am a writer.

Tim Harris. I believed I could be one when he said so.

Candy Finnigan. Who could have known that a nine-year-old card cheater would meet his future coauthor over heated rounds of Spite and Malice? You cheated too!

Candy and Sean wish to acknowledge:

Chris and Deb Finnigan, and their daughters, Molly and Erin. The Toledo Tribe lives on!

What a life, indeed!!

INDEX

Index

Index

Index

Parents
  guilt of, 9
  overprotectiveness of, 123
  seniors as, 151
Patches, of fentanyl, 43
Payment, 80, 81
Periodic alcoholic, 30–31
Phobias, 63
Physical symptoms, of detox, 21
Pill identification, 37
Pills.com, 37
Plastic surgery, addiction to, 68
Pornography, 64
  drug addiction with, 66
  treatment for, 67
Pot, 63
Prescription drugs. *See also* Over-the-
    counter drugs; Pain relievers
  adolescent use of, 38
  availability of, 40
  Internet identification of, 37
Privacy. *See also* Confidentiality
  of adolescents, 125
  eating disorders and, 67
Psychedelics, 56–57
Psychiatric treatment, 57. *See also*
    Spin-dry psychology
  for cutting, 66
  for eating disorders, 68
  for families, 160–61
  inpatient facility, 81
  Valium use in, 51
Psychosis, 92

Rape, Xanax's role in, 52
Raves, drug use at, 56
Reagan, Ronald, 166
Recovery, 1
  of adolescents, 141
  drug testing during, 165
  family, 110, 154, 155, 160–61
  language of, 10
  meetings after, 164

  priorities during, 168
  religion in, 159
  of seniors, 147, 150–51
  staff, status of, 81
Referrals, 81
Refusal, 120–21
Rehab. *See* Inpatient treatment
Relapse, 6, 168
  agreement creation and, 169
  causes of, 169–70
  consequences of, 171
  precursors to, 170
  Vicodin, 42
Relationships
  of adolescents, 132
  in intervention, 8–9
Religion, 2, 79, 159
Research. *See also* Information, sources of
  of drugs, 37
  on employment loss, 85
  of treatment, 68, 78–79
  of wilderness programs, 133
Resentment, 163
Residential treatment. *See* Inpatient
    treatment
Resources. *See also* Money
  financial, 16, 17, 80
  hotline, 20
  of information, 79
Restraining order, 158
Rights
  of adolescents, 125, 126
  treatment refusal, 71
Roman Catholics, intervention by, 2

Sal, story of, 75–76
School, attendance in, 62, 134
Secrecy. *See also* Privacy
  of addiction, 12–13, 112
  children and, 91
  in families, 139–40
  of spouse, 150
  treatment, 83–85

Index